Becoming

a call to love

To Mopsey from Janey with much love to you on your journey! ♡

Becoming

a call to love

Claire Blatchford

Lindisfarne Books

2004

Published by Lindisfarne Books
400 Main Street
Great Barrington, MA 01230
www.lindisfarne.org

Library of Congress Cataloging-in-Publication Data

Blatchford, Claire H.
Becoming : a call to love / Claire Blatchford.
p. cm.
ISBN 1-58420-022-7
I. Anthroposophy. 2. Spiritual life. I. Title.
BP596.S66B528 2004
299'.93 — dc22

10 9 8 7 6 5 4 3 2 1

Printed in the United States of America

Contents

FOR THE GUILFORD GROUP

past, present, yet to be

Introduction

THIS BOOK IS THE SEQUEL to *Turning* which was published in 1994. The words in *Turning* were heard inwardly between 1978-1981. The words in this book were received in like manner between 1991-1998. While the words in *Turning* were directed to me, the words in *Becoming* were directed not only to me but to a circle of friends with whom I was meeting regularly during that time.

In another book, *Friend of My Heart*, published in 1999, I attempted to describe the nature of my inner hearing. Sections from *Turning* and also from this new volume appear in *Friend of My Heart*. So if the reader has read *Friend of My Heart* he or she should not be surprised if some passages in here sound familiar. These passages are included because it is possible to experience the flow and power of the words that were given, quite apart from my own personal interpretations or elaborations on them. If, to speak metaphorically, *Friend of My Heart* can be compared to a description of a river, this sequel is an invitation to step into the river. It is my hope that by living with the words over time—reading, pondering and meditating on them—you will be stirred to walk, paddle, or swim upstream to discover the spring from which they come. True, the words in this volume came through me and were shaped by who I am yet the life in them is everywhere and most certainly within yourself. It is free for the asking and can, when given the chance, be found to quench thirst, soothe, jolt awake, wash clean and make new. Living water does not belong to any one place or person; by its very nature it must go on and ever on, changing in pace, depth, direction and composition as it goes. Thus, what has come to me in the form of words, may come to you in other forms: inspirations, imaginations, a simple, steady sense of gladness for life, moments of certainty of purpose and direction.

Even as there are different kinds of rivers—shallow, deep, swift, slow, straight, meandering—so are there different kinds of currents within both our exterior and interior lives. Who has not had the experience of being caught up in a bubbling onward rush of outer events or moods? And who has not experienced other times when, apart from what may be happening outwardly, one feels as though one is stranded on a sand bar? There is no question that our interior and exterior lives are intricately interwoven and what happens in one influences what happens in the other. Difficult or marvelous outer events can pull one's spirits down or raise them up. Inner moods can influence the entire course of a single day. In this book, however, as in *Turning*, it is the inner life that is seen to be foremost and of greatest importance. When speaking of inner life far more is meant than mere moods. All that manifests physically without in the world, be it idea, feeling, or activity, has had its beginning within, in the inner life. All that happens to us, no matter how unexpected or undeserved it may seem, is in some way connected to our innermost. It doesn't take clairvoyant powers to see these facts, only a willingness to look, to be honest, to care, and to begin to be responsible for the discoveries one makes. I have heard it said that even the condition of the earth is related to the movements of the human soul and spirit:

The elements reflect the intensity of what is to come.
Earthquake, flood, hurricane, tornado—
all are but outer whisps on the edge of inner movement.
Keep your eye on the light within
for the sake of your earth
as well as yourself.

Thus a growing awareness of and attentiveness to what goes on within our own soul and spirit can have a profound impact not only on our life and the lives of other people but on the earth too. It is not hard to see the connection between greedy thoughts and the impoverishment of the earth. Yet the implication in the above quotation is that *all* the elements, not just the ground beneath our feet, are responsive to our recognition of the elements within ourselves.

How can we become aware of and responsive to what goes on within without become overly self-involved? How can we live with confidence, faith, and power from the inside out rather than exclusively, as seems to be the case today, from the outside in? How—to continue the river metaphor—can we not only find but protect the inner stream of divine love and truth so its waters remain living, not stagnant or polluted waters channeled into self-serving projects?

An inner turning, as illustrated in the book under that name, represents for me the first step towards finding the answers to these questions. This turning must be understood as a "turning to" rather than a "turning away from." In the physical realm when we shift our vision from one thing to another we no longer see the thing we were looking at. In the spiritual realm something quite different happens: our vision expands to include not only the new but the old. When one turns, and keeps turning, to the spirit of the highest within oneself, opening to it with thankfulness, wonder, and trust, the spirit in the physical world not only becomes more evident everywhere, *it responds*. For this spirit of the highest within ourselves, the Christ spirit (the term is meant in a universal, not a sectarian sense), is not a distant spirit somewhere up in the heavens, it is within and all around, awaiting our recognition and participation. As I once heard:

If you can summon your spirit to see spirit,
the spirit outside responds.

My own experience of turning arose out of an inner longing and sense of expectancy. Beginning in my teens I had a recurring daydream of walking out the door of our house, or the dorm at college, or wherever I happened to be living at the time. I imagined going with nothing more than the clothes I was wearing, and walking on and on into some "other" landscape which I sensed was there, but had not yet found my way into. This was not an urge to run away; I already knew that the ups and downs of my life were with me wherever I went. Then in 1978 a clairvoyant friend told me that "someone" wanted to meet me (as described in greater detail in *Friend of My Heart*) and I experienced the inner turning. I turned from my ordinary, every day way of thinking and perceiving to the "someone" within who offered a truly spiritual way of thinking and perceiving both myself and the world. Looking back now I realize the daydream ended at this time. I had lived right into it.

I believe this first step, this turning, is different for every person, whether it be prompted by longing and expectancy, through significant encounters with others, or through dramatic sometimes painful outer events. I believe, too, that it can occur as quietly and gently as a leaf floating around a river bend. *Turning* did make me more self-conscious, more self-aware, but not, I trust, in a narcissistic way. If the experience of turning is genuine you sense, above all, the presence of love. You *know* through and through, beyond any mental understanding, that you are loved exactly as you are. I, myself, felt filled to overflowing with gladness. No other words can describe it. But a true turning is not a mere, transitory emotional high, a "feeling good about yourself and the world," it presents a challenge. The challenge is expressed in these words:

Look and listen—
Rouse yourself to go at once beyond yourself
(your worries, fears and doubts)
and to enter truly into yourself, into your center,
wherein is the spirit, the I AM.

Turning can be called not only an awakening but a baptism in the river of paradox. While you discover you are loved as you are, and this discovery can bring a genuine inner calm free of the need to prove yourself to the world, you also know you are nowhere near being all you can be. You are exalted *and* humbled. You awaken to the light *and* the darkness. And it can happen that while the love you are experiencing within is truly wonderful, things without can suddenly seem to become more difficult. My own understanding of this, from my experience, is that love within not only calls forth love without, it can also call forth fear.

We come now to the second step needed to answer the questions raised earlier, as to how we can live from out of our highest, innermost spirit continuously amid the wear, tear, distractions, the very mundaneness of everyday outer life. That is the purpose of this sequel. *Becoming* is about entering into and making real the connection we've made through the act of turning to the Christ spirit. It is about realizing the power of commitment to and trust in this spirit within and what it may tell or show us, regardless of what the world without is saying.

I truly believe that the spirit of the highest awaits our recognition and participation. If this spirit is compared to a moving river, you may wonder how flowing waters can "wait" for us. While the spirit is always in motion—and motion in the spirit realm does not necessarily mean constant activity and restlessness such as we may associate with motion in the physical realm—its "livingness" depends to a large degree on our receptivity to it. If we are connected to living waters we have no wish to be dead-end recipients of divine grace. We recognize that being able to receive means being willing to let go. We recognize that we can't be filled up if we are already full, nor can we be carried along if we are holding on. Most wonderful of all we recognize that the spirit responds to this willingness by calling forth yet more of itself, giving more without any reserve, and carrying us through ever more wonderful landscapes. These thoughts are best expressed by the spirit itself:

As my light enters you and you pass it on,
it isn't used up.
Quite the opposite,
more light is generated.

~

There is no such thing as creating out of nothing.
God created out of Himself,
and needs you to create Himself further out of yourselves.
When this fails to happen there is a build up of forces
that can't flow and express themselves.
Wars and disasters can help set things in motion again.

John F. Gardner, in his introduction to the first edition of *Turning*, advised that that book "not be read in 'logical'" sequence, from first page to last" but that it be opened at seeming random as need arose. Many people have followed this advice and, as a result, I have heard story after story of the exact right help and comfort being found on the page opened to. I believe a similar procedure can be followed with this sequel.

A variation on this idea of opening at random is to turn to the table of contents and read where one feels guided. You will see that the messages have been arranged in sixteen chapters, each having to do with a certain theme or way of being. The words were not received in this order, I was told to gather them together in this way to intensify their effect. Each chapter could be said to be a current, or strand, within the larger river of which we have been speaking. Even as various currents branch off from the most forward moving part of a river and flow through different spaces before returning to the main channel, so is it with these chapters. This must be understood as being a characteristic of the interior life. As was once explained to me:

> The spiritual life does not progress in a straight line.
> Events don't occur in A-B-C order.
> Think of the water in the river,
> swirling,
> folding back over itself,
> working its way onwards in patterns.
> Movements rise up within and are created as well
> by the river banks or objects in the water.
> Seek to flow with me,
> with my love,
> with the All.
> Be not afraid.
> Later you'll see the pattern,
> you'll see how the spirit in you knew all along
> where it was going.

Thus, when looking over the table of contents, you may find yourself drawn to a particular chapter. Or you might close your eyes and let your circling finger direct you to the one that will speak to your needs.

It has often come to my attention that there is a repetitious nature to many of the thoughts I've heard within. I am, for example, told over and over to be thankful. I used to feel like a dull-witted clod whenever I realized, "I've heard this before." Now I know there is a more grateful and gracious way to view this. The Christ spirit, when we open to it, really does work on us in waves that come and go, move this way and that way, and sometimes withdraw altogether in order that we may realize we actually are clods without it. It knows better than we what we need and, with a nudge, push, or pull in this direction or that, seeks to help us shape ourselves day by day, inch by inch. Sometimes it leads us through lush, verdant pastures of praise, other times it forces us up against hard walls of honesty, but the living essence of it is always love. Love that pours itself out endlessly, selflessly, abundantly. Love that would have us become what we in our inmost and truest selves long to become.

Claire Blatchford

Be in the right here, right now

I need you as you are, right now, right here.
Don't waste time trying to fix up everything in yourself.
Give up your regrets, doubts, worries, fears,
let your sole intention be:

> I am here
> O Lord my God.

~

You want to get through with one thing and on to the next;
combat this tendency.
Strive to be fully and lovingly in the *now*.

~

You must be able, in your quiet time,
to bring your thoughts quickly
to the point where you want to be—
with me.
Turn from the lazy, the unsure, the stumbling, the protesting,
the ever-so-busy voices,
to me.

~

You know,
through the dark or light of your feelings,
when you are near my heart.
Listen and watch.
Your soul's wish must be not merely to sense my heart
but to *grow* into it.
Momentary happiness is not enough.
Your soul longs as never before
to dwell in the light,
to be shaped and led by it,
for it knows there is no other way.

~

Only in the right here, right now can you find
peace, love, joy, inspiration, and courage.

Stop, drop all,
come unto me.
I am the right now, right here!

Stop blaming yourself,
stop looking for the fault in yourself,
just accept what comes,
as it comes.
Don't expect more
or less.
Don't be disappointed.

Give thanks for every crumb that is given.
This way you will learn
true self-less-ness.

⁓

Feed on the thought of my presence.
Don't pick and nibble,
don't let it just be a thought,   ✓
take it in deeply,
feel it through your whole being.

⁓

To the degree that you aren't here—
are elsewhere in thought and attention—
you are stealing from yourself.

⁓

Too often you want to "get through things."
To what?
Give thanks for where you are *in this very moment.*
It will help recollect you, open you to the little things
    you're missing.
It will be food for those on the other side
many of whom suffer because they rushed through their
    earthly lives.
When you do what they did not do, it is balm for them.

Don't get all caught up
in thinking about what you have to do,
that will exhaust you.
Believe you have all the time you need,
trust that all the strength you need will be there,
have faith in my very near presence and help.

I am right here,
breath of your breath,
heart of your heart.

Being expectant is different from expecting messages,
expecting to fill up this notebook,
expecting to have something to show for your efforts.

Try today to be quiet and joyfully expectant,
open to me and to Our Father
in everything.
Find your messages in the daily events,
in others,
in the earth and sky.

~

What you want and need is right here,
not over there
or in some abstract future.
Drink of me,
drink of my light and love,
drink of my heart,
drink through your eyes, ears, throat.

~

I want to live through you
in this moment.
Are you willing to suspend your own wants,
turn a deaf ear to fears and doubts,
and do what you know you ought to do?
Are you willing to stand naked —totally naked?
If you can do it with gladness,
I will meet you there
in the open spot you have created,
and another kind of work will begin.

~

When you can find me
right where you are,
both inwardly and outwardly,
in joy and sorrow,

in clarity and confusion,
my light will,
like the sun
rise and rise.
See it rising
in the faces of those you love.
See it rising when all looks dark.

For I am in your world.
I am everywhere you choose to be.
I am in your public and private moments,
your ins and outs,
your waking and sleeping.

Dear heart, allow my light to grow ever brighter,
allow it to rise up from below to hold you,
ray out from above to guide you,
surround and protect you,
right here, right now.

Enter into the silence

Lay down the restless, impatient feelings.
Allow yourself to wait.
Allow yourself to be in the silence.

⁓

To be able to enter daily into the silence
without worries, fears, doubts,
without plans of any sort,
to say no more than, "I am here"
and feel it is so,
simply and truly,
that is an act of faith,
an exercise in openness, nakedness, attentiveness, devotion.
It will shape your soul to meet me.

⁓

It is of the utmost importance
that you maintain the sanctuary within,
wherever you are.
Then I can come, rest,
and be with others through you.

Enter the place where you are not propped up by thoughts.
Enter into silence and belief.
Belief is the spine,
holding you upright.
It goes down beyond thought
and reaches up into truth.

Focus on this spine of light.
moving down in faith,
up in hope.

Enter the place where your heart,
your center,
is completely open to heavenly thought.
Open yourself to the imprint of Divine thought and love.
Love-thought enters your entire being,
not just your head.

The sacred silence is the field
where the inner voice takes root and grows.
It needs to be cultivated.
One must love and enjoy this work.
Don't dread it,
or regard it as duty and obligation.
In the end your life depends on it,

for from it springs—
my bread,
manna from me to you.
Silence and inner space are closely related.
In the inner space
you meet the largeness and closeness of the divine.

~

Attempt in silence and simplicity
to do your best daily.
Know I am beside you.

Be open, empty, hungry,
expectant, trusting

Do not be afraid to be an empty vessel.
Keep focused on me and my light,
you will be filled at the right time.

~

You want the flood of light, contact, and insight,
you forget that work is needed to get there.
To open, and remain open, is hard work.
To come again and again to the point of selflessness and
      nothingness—
which is not really nothingness though it may seem so—
requires work.
Through selflessness, namelessness, nothingness
you begin to acquire fluidity.

~

Your emptiness is your treasure.

Don't think, "Ah! That's a paradox!"
Go into this thought.

Explore it, become familiar with it in every way.
To the degree that you can empty out
and hold yourself open, expectant, and glad,
you will be filled.
Pay no attention to the negative thoughts that try to crowd in,
tell them to leave.

～

Inner action *always* leads to outer movement.

～

You cannot be too careful in what you say to others.
The more authority you are given,
the more power in your words.

Seek greater stillness, purer silence.
Give up all ambition to receive for others.
You are useful to the extent
that you are without ambition,
without plans and hopes of your own.
You are useful to the extent
that you are glad, open, and single of eye.

Silence the overly curious, questioning mind.
Give where you are—whole heartedly—
to all that you come into contact with.

Learn to be in the not-knowing-where-you-are-going.
Learn to draw closer to me—
always, everywhere,
in all ways.

~

Root out all spiritual ambition.

Q: How, Lord?

Go naked,
there is no other way.
And give thanks.

~

I want to live through you
in this moment.
Are you willing to suspend your own wants,
to turn a deaf ear to fears, doubt,
and to what you feel you ought to do?
Are you willing to stand naked—totally naked?
If you can do it in gladness
I will meet you there
in the open spot you have created,
and another kind of work will begin.

I don't want you doing mental gymnastics around other people.
What's the point in that?
To impress them?
Learn to stand still when others can't be still.
Learn to go naked while others dress up.

When you begin to think you have found the way
          into the spiritual worlds,
it is taken from you.
For you there is only one way,
the way of emptiness,
letting go,
daring to stand alone,
trusting that Our Father is there,
no matter the deafness, blindness, confusion.

Don't be afraid of the emptiness,
the feeling of lack of direction and purpose.
You have to learn to be comfortable in it
before the way can really emerge.

The only way you can hold close to me is through the cultivation
of an attitude of openness and humility,
being willing to admit you don't know,
being willing to turn from your mental "knowing"
to the unexpected and unknown.
Let me flow into you
rather than claiming, "Christ says this or that."

Let this become an activity of the heart.
You are ever new, ever young,
ever filled with joy, strength, and clarity
when my light is working through you.

Feed on me.
Go from me
and return to me
in everything.
There is no other way.
You cannot eat tomorrow's supper now
and not need something tomorrow.
Let me be ever fresh in you
Not a left-over.

If you can feed on me
others can too.

(Others have done it and are doing it now.)
Know in all humility
that your experience of me isn't the all,
yet the all cannot exist without your small part in it.

⁓

Act in faith even if your acting has to be a waiting.
How does one "act" in waiting?
By being open, being *all* there,
by being expectant in faith.

⁓

Allow yourself to be uncertain about outcomes, directions,
    and so forth.
Allow yourself to live in the uncertainties,
to flow and not be fearful.
Say, "It's okay if things are bumpy and there are difficulties.
It's okay as long as I am centered in my Lord."

⁓

Stop grasping,
learn to be in uncertainty and doubt,
without loosing gladness.
Don't eat more than you need.

Although you know what you want to do
and feel you should do,
although you have the energy and enthusiasm for it,
and it is good,
be ready to drop even that,
and to come
in openness and humility to me.

Trust.
Trust in your own growth,
and in the growth of your loved ones.
Trust that your way will unfold,
and the way of those you love will unfold,
maybe not beautifully, but truly.
Trust that all will work together for the love of God.

To trust,
and in trusting remain ever open and unburdened
by the weight of your own known and unknown errors
     is essential.
Trust with child-like trust
that your father is there,
ready to catch you every time you fall.

And yet you must be ever vigilant,
ever ready to recognize and admit error.

You don't even need to try to sort out the feelings,
let go of them,
give them to me,
move on.

Trust—
don't hurry,
don't strain,
act with trust.

Drop the old stories.
Drop the need to be somebody with definite work.
Discover what a relief it is to step forward into the *now*,
into each moment unadorned,
alive only to the heart,
to the knowing in the heart that can be quickened,
through which I can speak
and long to speak.

Go past the fear of being nobody,
to being totally present in the here and now.

~

Your emptiness will become fullness,
your waiting will become a blooming,
your aloneness will become an all-at-oneness.
Be patient, dear soul,
keep your eye on the light
and your heart ever ready.

~

Do not fear,
always be glad,
keep your eye on the light
and the ear in your heart ever open.
The sense of expectancy is so important.
You need not tell others of it,
you can hold it within,
hold and cherish it
and simply open to what comes
without fuss or fanfare.

Be silent in the expectancy.
Do not fear the times when nothing seems to be happening or
    coming.
What is wrong with living in a great expectancy?
Is not expectancy a light in itself,
a beacon leading you into the future?

Drop what others have said,
thoughts from the books you've read,
go back into the hunger—
let it guide you.
Let the hunger call up the outline
of what I have to give you,
then you will be fed.
Don't look back,
keep going straight on ahead.

Don't plan everything.
Let the spirit educate and lead you.
Your job is to be flexible, open, wondering, glad.

You want to be told you're going in the "right" direction
so you can proceed—
right?
Drop the need to be right.
Drop the need to be going, moving, doing;
attempt to enter into the other dimension,
that of be-ing.

Q: How, Lord?

Be in me.
Be in all you love.
If you don't know what it's like to be in me,
then all your going is pointless running about.

Q: Lord, help me to be in you.

You can't have the being-in-me
for once and for all.
The concept of owning it
is as pointless
as that of running towards it,
or of trying to be "right."
It is as simple and wholesome as laughter.
What's the joke here?
Open into it
without the mental grasping
for the punch line.
Open unto it,
be in it,
in me,
right here.

Think of it all as an adventure,
an attitude, a listening for me and Our Father.

Delight in not knowing where I will lead you,
what I will show you,
trusting always that I am with you.
You worry you'll be scattered here and there,
no definite, lasting, substantial thoughts to hold onto
or follow,
you say it all seems so random.

Trust me.
Through trust
rest in me.
Seek to know me.
And I will lead you into the only way,
the lasting way of thinking.

Come unto me.

~

If you doubt yourself you cannot create yourself.
You are doubting the highest, that which longs to create.
Does the gardener doubt the seeds she puts in the earth?
Does the cook doubt the yeast he mixes with the flour?
Does the painter doubt the colors she works with?
Attempt periodically to weed out all self-doubt.

~

(These words rose up in my heart and were with me for several days, like a song, "You, Christ, are the reason for my being." They were answered ...)

And you, dear heart,
are the reason for my being.
If only *every* heart
would open to me!

(The tone became lighter ...)
I am looping you in,
drawing you ever closer.
I have lassoed you with love!

~

It's important
after you have entered into your knowing
that you give it back to the universe
and become a new unknowing
but ever open heart.

~

Must there always be a thought?
Must you always have something to ponder?
Why can't the thought be simply your bodily-felt sense
of the goodness of where you are in this moment?
Let that be all.
Let it flow.

No need to catch hold of everything.
Open your hands skyward,
let them reflect the heavens.
Let your heart reflect the sun.
Be the song you feel
vibrating through your body.

~

You see the roses opening and opening.
The color, the shapes, the fragrance stir in you too.
From out of the dark,
from out of thorny stems,
from out of deep patience and time
these come forth.
Yes, you see the blossoming of the seed.
Do not forget what went into it,
what must be offered,
cared for,
pruned and watered.
If every soul you love is to come forth into flower
much must come to pass.
Do not question that the blossom will ever appear
simply because you do not know
from where the other forces will come.
They *will* come.
Karmic turnings both painful and strengthening.

~

All I ask
is that you be ever hopeful,
ever open,
ever ready to look
for the truly loving way.

The need to achieve
even if it is for me —
let that go.
Let my light in you
lead the way.

~

(During a Sunday service, at the start of communion.)

Look at this little piece of bread:
you eat a lot more than that when you eat every day,
don't you?
But this little piece of bread, taken in My Name,
can fill you,
can be everything,
can open you in ways you hardly realize.
You do not need great slices of me,
indeed, that would be more than you could bear.
Just a little bit of me
can go a long way in bringing grace and light

into all you do, think, and say.
Remember to turn daily to the little bit of me
that you can take, eat, and absorb.
Because it seems small (10 minutes, 15 minutes, 30 minutes)
it may seem unimportant,
may be easily forgotten,
but without it you can shrivel up and waste away.

~

Keep light.
Stay open.
Keep listening.
Stay quiet.

Wait for the knowing in the heart,
yet move ever on.
Rest in me,
yet have no home.

Be ever glad

Attitude is everything!
Gratitude, expectancy, trust ...
Let them resound within.

~

I have said many times you are not alone.
I am not the only one who is near;
many more than you realize are near,
are watching and listening with interest.
Many are waiting—as Paul knew—
on tip toe.
Be glad, ever so glad!
Give all you can to where you are.

~

You have so much to work with.
Give thanks!
And trust,
trust the inner flashes of knowing.

Look out into the world,
give thanks,
look and listen.

Then—
look into the world within,
give thanks,
look and listen.
Hold up all to my light for transformation.
Keep it simple.

Give thanks for your dear daily bread,
for that which is given to you to do,
which only you can do,
which feeds you as you do it
and, in turn, helps to feed others.

Be it fancy or plain,
sweet or tart,
fresh or stale,
small in portion or large,
be glad for the work that is set before you.
Take, eat,
and know as you eat
that you are one with all life.

~

Attempt to draw sweetness from the great spaces—
from the clouds, the mountains, the rivers and flowers.
Open up and out.
Be glad!
Let beauty flow into you
that it may flow on to others in service.

~

Enjoy life!
Enjoy every person you are with,
listen for me in that person.
Enjoy all that your eyes rest on.
Feel the enjoyment, the appreciation going forth
as from a hidden spring.

~

Learn to take others into your heart in gladness,
without weariness or sadness.
I will teach you this.
I need you unencumbered.

~

Don't wait until you are in the center of gratitude.
Don't leave it to chance.
Know how to enter into it fully, in real consciousness.

Q: How Lord?

Look right where you are for spirit
in even the simplest and smallest of things:
stone, leaf, flower, cloud,
in every face you look into,
every smile,
every wag of your dog's tail.

If you can summon your spirit to seek spirit,
the spirit outside responds.
When spirit meets spirit,
gratitude is born.

~

Seek ever new ways
in which to express the spirit of gratitude and praise.

~

Suppress your own wanting for now.
Suppress the questions,
just rest in me.
And then the deeper wanting,
the deeper questions
will rise up
and gush forth in true gladness.

~

Shift your perception from what you, yourself, want to
    achieve
to what the spirit in you longs to achieve and perceive.
Align yourself to the becoming,
to the coming of spirit,
through gladness and gratitude.

~

Rejoice!
Rejoice in the knowledge
that my word can be heard in the heart
of every man and woman!
Where one is,
how old one is,
what language one speaks,
what one does,
the schooling one has had—
they make no difference.
All souls centered in me are one.

~

Every wish from your heart,
every true prayer you send heavenwards
is taken by the angels,
is heard—
is lovingly taken—

is like a seed that may, in their care, later bear great fruit.
Be glad.
Do not cease praying from your heart ever.
Continue to give thanks for that which you cannot yet see.
You are seen.
You are heard.
Let your heart be true and earnest in its seeking.
Give it full rein,
it knows the way.

Be honest

Focus on the essential.
Be honest about this.
You allow yourself to get caught up too easily
in unimportant things.

~

More than gratitude must be cultivated,
more than faith.
Total honesty is needed
if the heart is to be pure.

Transform your ambition
through scrupulous honesty
and you will find the way
not only outwardly but within.

Q: Will I have to listen to this over and over until I am
transformed?

Until you've mastered it.
Come on—
dance through the darkness,

dip, bend, and twirl back into the light.
Movement is the key
as long as you don't allow it to become rootlessness, scatteredness.

Do you want most to work with me?
Are you fooling yourself?
Why do you keep thinking you can get things done without
    my help?
Are you afraid that what *I* want is not going to be what *you* want?
Can you answer these questions honestly?

See—you haven't yet come into the full reality of me.

Are you allowing fear and worry to rule you?

All right—your fears—
What are they?
Where are they?
How did you come by them?
List them—
get them out there
where you can see them.
Discover how unnecessary they are,
and give them to me.

49

It's good that you can be honest with yourself.
Just be careful, as you seek to open through honesty,
that you don't also open to discouragement.
Ask that my light be with you.

There are many delicate soul processes you can become
conscious of and attuned to.
By becoming aware of them you can participate in them
and help to change them.
Don't force awareness through the use of stimulants,
regard your ambitions with reserve,
when nothing seems to be forthcoming don't get discouraged.
Fight discouragement,
turn from it and face my light,
speak to my light as you would to a trusted friend.
Invite it in,
ask it to lead you through your day
and out into the spiritual worlds all around.
Don't be afraid to be with the so-called dead.
They are closer than you realize,
their influence in your life
is greater than you realize.
Send thanks to them.

Seek more than soul knowledge,
open to spirit knowledge
for the two are closely entwined.

Soul knowledge can lead right into spirit knowledge,
but many today stop at soul knowledge,
they never see the opening
of the small self into the great spirit.
Others want only spirit knowledge,
the blossoms and the fruits,
they forget about the roots, trunk, branches, twigs, leaves.

Soul and body are needed
if the spirit is to blossom and bear fruit.
True self-knowledge unfolds into spirit knowledge.
It raises the small self into the universal self,
strengthening and completing it.

Self-knowledge—as in soul knowledge—
is only a step towards the true,
the truly needed knowledge
which is spirit knowledge.

I am here not only to help you find soul knowledge,
but spirit knowledge as well.
I am here to help you enter into spirit knowledge,
and *use* it.

~

Don't allow yourself to get caught up in the wanting,
the head wanting and the greed.
Yes, there are seven deadly sins
that prevent you from being with me.
The root of them all is the same,
it's ingratitude.

To think you can "own" love—nonsense!
Love lives only in the giving.
If "owned" it becomes lifeless.

~

You are all "head-wanting" today, not "heart-longing."
You feel it and are ashamed.
It's good that you recognize the difference.
Lose yourself and your small head-wanting in gratitude,
in praise,
in appreciation of the incredible complexity of the higher
    worlds
while knowing it is also very simple.
Let that humble you.
As you awaken the light within and awaken to it,
as you create yourself in asking, in prayer, in giving, in adoration,
so is everything else around you created.
If you could see with the eyes of the spirit you would see this.
This is of the future,

this creating with light,
with love and joy,
with me.

~

Let not your concern be
"What can the world do for me
that I may be someone in it?"
But rather,
"What can I do for the world?"

Pay attention to which way the current is going—
sucking inwards in wanting,
or flowing outwards in giving.

~

Stop making resolutions you can't keep.
Know yourself.
Be fair with yourself.

~

Stay alert,
do not get caught up in spiritual glamour.

~

The whole way you think about your children from minute to
     minute
can make an enormous difference.
It can be the difference between helping them and harming them!

⁓

Mary learned not to interfere,
so must you,
so must every mother.

⁓

Part of the task of coming into true consciousness
is recognizing how imperative it is
that it be consciousness *in me*,
not in any form of fantasy.

Q: How can I know?

It's a matter of the heart, not the head.
You can strive with your head to create pictures
and you can convince yourself you are in these pictures
     and they are real,
when in truth you are entirely off the mark.
True consciousness occurs in the heart.
Strength lies in being able to start fresh every time,
asking out of real need and devotion.
Those are your markers.

You know in your heart
when you're at the bottom,
lost and starved.
Real need cannot be set up,
cannot be pretended by the honest heart.
The same goes for devotion.
Your heart *knows* the difference between sentimental piety
and true adoration.

Q: What about the times when I'm "stuck" in busy thoughts
or in complaints or depression?

You will recognize them for their value.
Darkness has its value.
Instead of tossing about
you can learn to accept and endure.
That you have *all* time to get where you need to go
and yet live in *no* time, in the eternal,
is dawning on you.

Rest in the eternal despite outer and inner pressures.
If you can do this you will be helping the dead also
who crowd in on the other side.
Such resting can give you poise,
the poise to say, "Yes" or "No",
"Come" or "Go."
In my consciousness there is this poise,
this perfect resting between dark and light.

Move in full trust
into my wisdom, love, protection, and joy.
Let not your heart be fearful,
let it not be impatient,
let it not be discouraged—
I am close.

～

Before every wish ask yourself:
"Is this for the higher or the lower?"
If for the higher,
take it, claim it, *do* it.
If for the lower,
give it up,
give that part of yourself up to me.
I will take it, transform it
and will pour the light from it
not only over your life
but over the lives of all
who are near you.

～

There is a race to run.
Don't lose time doing warm-ups
or trying to figure out what shoes to wear.
Don't suddenly wander off the track.
How odd, how pathetic that would be

if an Olympian runner suddenly strolled off course
to look at something,
have a drink, or whatever.

~

(I said I felt unworthy.)

Okay, fine, you *are* unworthy,
that's why I'm with you.
Why beat yourself?
When you do that it's as though somewhere within
you really think you are worthy.
Cut the crap!
Pride has three faces, not one.
Learn to recognize all of them.

~

You have to be willing to go back to Round One anytime.

(I said I thought that was the case.)

Apparently not.
The angels read your soul and see that isn't the case.

(I said, "Okay, back to Round One. What else is new?")

(Then I heard laughter.)

Why go to that minister to find answers to questions about me
and your relationship with me?
Can't we find the answers together?
Dear heart, I love you
and I know you love me,
yet there's this difficulty of entrusting yourself completely
to me.

The hard work comes *after* the vision.
Give up entirely your "outer" ideas of what you want and expect,
have only the inner expectation,
the hope of connecting with me
and working with me.
Let the outer unfold from that.

Loosen up,
lighten up,
and the look you don't like on your own face—
which you feel even if you can't see it—
will disappear.

So many of your "stresses" become laughable
when you see them in my light.

~

The minute you begin to be against something
in critical thought or feeling
you cut yourself off from it.
Don't waste energy cutting yourself off.
Those of like spirit need one another
though they may never even meet on the physical plane.
As my spirit moves in you so will it move in others
eventually drawing all together in one great stream.

~

Be willing to let go of words and thoughts
no matter how true and beautiful they sound.

~

Banish all thoughts of power from your mind and soul.
ask them to leave.

This includes fantasies
that arise of having others come to you for advice or healing.

The truth of the matter is:
you cannot advise or heal.

Love all who come your way,
only love can lead you where you must go.

~

There's a limit to housecleaning.
Some become so obsessed with it
they never hear my knock at the door.
Stop beating yourself,
stop asking the impossible of yourself.
Just turn from that self to me,
simply, easily.
Let me surprise you out of yourself.

~

Forget the way you think you should be,
remember to love yourself as you are.

~

You must give up wanting to change people,
you cannot counsel anyone till you've done that.

~

Hold to what you are *for* —
in every person and situation,
in every moment,
not what you are against.

~

He whom you look down upon in impatience or pride,
becomes your stumbling stone and your judge.
Learn from all men,
specially those you stumble on!

~

The more you attempt to work for me,
the harder kicks your small ego.
Recognize this and through recognition combat it.

~

That's your ego squealing,
turning and twisting,
wanting to know what's going on,
demanding a place, a title!

It's what all have to shed
to let themselves be—
in silence,
in emptiness
(how the ego fears emptiness!)
Then I can enter
softly, quietly ...

~

Admit your error and go on.
What's the big deal?
You know many of your weak spots already,
accept them, give thanks, and go on.

~

Don't fret.
Be willing to expand
in gratitude and in patience.
Be willing to begin again,
ever and again.

~

Become aware of the "dry" times.
Recognize them and fortify yourself
in the realization that they are necessary.

~

Quit scratching!
Quit trying to reply to everything that comes at you.
Give up the urge to be right,
or to get even with others.
Words can become traps and treadmills.
Just turn to my light
and ask that it open you,
enter, warm, and enlarge you.

Resolve to say no word that adds to the scratching.
Be silent
until the right words come to you.

I have no wish to scold you,
you do a good enough job of that on yourself.
Just don't get too caught up in it.

Breathe deeper and deeper
in the *I AM*
that you may become steadier, surer.

You can just drop the feelings of failure
and enter into my peace.
Drop them and be renewed.
I don't look at the failures.
I look at the gift you bring when you come,
which is yourself.
To be concerned about failure is to stay wrapped up in self.
So drop that and come,
specially when you feel empty, worthless, exhausted.

Every lie you make,
no matter how small,
dims your view of the spiritual world
and distorts your hearing.

Exaggerations can be lies.
As you get to know yourself
you know when they are playful nothings
and when they have crossed the line
between embellishment and dishonesty.

~

You are continually failing the spiritual world,
failing it in-so-far as you give in to the demands
and whims of the lower,
the lesser ego.
Yet this very failing is the door to an opening
in-so-far as you are willing to humbly admit this tendency to fail.

~

Why look longingly at the form of another person's life?
Appreciate it, give thanks for it,
but don't long for it for yourself.
That is taking away from yourself,
belittling, neglecting, stealing—
When you do that you fail to see
what can come to you,
what can shape you.
You fail to see the love that waits to shape you.

~

Shame can be the beginning of wisdom,
so don't be ashamed of it.

~

No matter what is happening outwardly,
no matter how you are feeling inwardly,
seek to remain true to the central core of yourself.
That you remain true to this core
is what is important in any relationship with anyone.
Seek to know the core ever more intimately and quickly.
It is the place in which your true note arises.
It is also the place where the true questions arise
and, in turn, the true answers.

If you feel impoverished
return to this core.
If confused or fearful,
return there.
It is the door into the highest in you
leading to me.

Others can wander
right by their inner core,
but if you are true to yours,
you will help them find their own.

Ask yourself every now and then,
"Where is my core?
Am I anywhere near it?"

As you come into your core, your center,
into me
so will you find passage into other realms,
into other hearts.

⁓

You must learn not to take it personally
when you receive nothing for long stretches of time.
Not only because the spiritual world
may, quite simply, have nothing to share,
or because it has chosen some other route than you
(this is nothing to be dismayed about for all, eventually,
        become one),
but because you need to be yet more objective.

It is good and important
not only to be honest with the spiritual world and yourself.
It is good, also, to be able to say, "So be it"
with patience and thankfulness.

⁓

It is all a matter of waking up to the inner world,
to the eternal,

to the spirit that moves in all things
and of recognizing one's place in it.

Stop and ask yourself every now and then,
"Are these thoughts in me active or reactive?"
If truly active,
then alive,
creative and open to love and truth.
If reactive,
then dead,
down-pulling,
separating.
To react is to separate.

If you cannot come to prayer in the spirit of love,
do not come.
"In the spirit of love" does not only mean in the spirit of gladness.
You can be sad,
you can be fearful or doubtful,
yet you can come in the spirit of love.
When you are in the spirit of love
you know I who love you am near.
You are faithful and trusting in the spirit of love.
If the spirit is one of indifference, cynicism or doubt
you are not in the spirit of love.

Clean yourself before coming
by being honest,
leaving petty concerns and worries behind,
going naked.

~

Discouragement, doubt, dissension, greed ...
there is *nothing* straightforward about them.
They can worm their way into you,
you are never immune to them,

they can affect you right down into your physical body
without being aware of them.

The greater your faith
the more subtle they become.
Yet the deeper your faith in me,
the greater the victory,
and the purer the light that will shine forth from you.
So remain alert.
Alert in thankfulness,
truthfulness and straightforwardness
with yourself and with others,
alert in your own simple efforts
at giving love and seeking truth.

~

Just keep going,
don't attempt to rid yourself of your past,
as though it were evil.
Some day you'll look back
and see the darkness you've been through.
Even darkness has it purpose and beauty.

~

You will always fail, again and again.
You will sleep and wake, and sleep again.
So it is with all human beings.
It is a part of being where and as you are.
Do not fight it,
accept it and do not stop—ever!

Come now,
stand again in hope and faith.
Pick up and go on.

~

The wisdom you win through to
must not become canned,
it must be ever fresh
for life to go on.

~

There is no other way
but through stop-start, test, advance-retreat
of your *whole* being.
Let yourself become an instrument for divine music,
yet keep your feet on the earth.
Strive to be fully conscious
not only of yourself as an instrument
that needs to be tuned, cared for, and polished,
be conscious of the music and its meaning.

～

Nothing can manifest outwardly
until you are so sure
so anchored in the inner,
through what you see in the inner,
that you know the outer
to be but a shadow of the real.

～

It is *very good* that, together, you can admit you don't know
what the task is,
what the way is.
Two or more souls gathered together in my name,
freely admitting ignorance,
yet trusting and hoping,

this means that two or more did not sleep
when I prayed in Gethsemane.
You can't understand this now
but it is so.

Daily I pray as in Gethsemane
and souls sleep
in promises they can't keep,
in thoughts that chain them to the earth,
in deeds that lead nowhere.

Be of good courage

Reach out and claim what is yours.
Don't say "I would like,"
dare to say *"I am."*
"I am creating …"
"I am seeking …"
"I am loving …"
Dare to take big steps in creating, seeking and loving yourself,
your true self.
Turn away from, "Maybe" and "If it is meant to be."
Be more assertive.
Trust that I will be with you
even if you're off the track,
even if you have to crash into a stone wall
before hearing me.

~

How do you feel the "I" in your own I am?
Is it a shout or a whisper?
Is it stiff or supple,
young or old?
What color is it?
Can you feel how it changes colors and shapes

yet remains the same?
Do not be afraid to define yourself
in the most wonderful ways you can imagine.
The I am is without end,
without limitations.
It is *me* in you
waiting to be discovered
not just once but again and again.

⁓

Listen carefully,
for I would have you rest near my heart,
and go out daily in the world from there.
This is the new way.

⁓

Fear puts up walls where no walls are necessary.

⁓

Can you begin to comprehend the thought
that you are not alone, are *never* alone,
even when you don't hear from me?
You are a part of the larger body of humanity,
an important part.
Every part of the body has a purpose.

~

"What is the most courageous thing I can do or think today?"
Ask yourself daily.

~

You must *ask* and *take!*
Don't hesitate, don't doubt—
Take!

Take light,
take faith,
take hope,
move forward.

~

Believe in and follow the essential simplicity and directness
of your own soul.
It knows the way.

~

You cannot be of real service to anyone
unless you are able to give up your children, your friends,
    all security.

~

Live for ideas and ideals not for personal relationships.
Let the relationships grow out of the ideas and ideals.

~

You must not always want closeness,
connectedness with your fellow human beings.
Be prepared to walk the open stretches by yourself,
knowing that the spirit sings all around,
though your hearing may be dulled by doubt,
and your vision dimmed by shadows.

~

Your heart's intention must be simple and straightforward.
It doesn't necessarily follow however
that the path is simple and straightforward.

The seed longs from deep in the earth
to grow into the light of the sun
but there may be obstacles of many sorts
around and through which it must grow
to get closer to the sun.

The sun and that which vibrates to it within the heart,
they are simple and straightforward.
The obstacles which keep the two apart
help the heart to find its true strength and courage
without which it cannot grow straight and strong.

~

Look straight ahead,
move as your heart directs you,
be not afraid of apparent outer failure.
The thought of your work for me
should be so alive
it will overcome the gravity of other people's doubt.

∽

Seek my light inwardly.
Face it.
Ask it to wash you clean.
This can hurt,
can even burn.
But be not afraid,
be of good courage,
let my light transform you.

∽

There are times when each of you
must travel alone into the wilderness,
into the unidentified, unmarked, dark spaces
in order to shift through the past and the present,
the known and unknown,
the necessary and not so necessary.
Do not be frightened by these places,
where familiar points recede and become like a mirage.
Just hold close to the thought:

Father, I praise and bless you,
I love you with all my being,
lead me where you would have me go.

~

The plus side of confusion
is that you're attempting to grow
into something larger.
Don't worry about being right or doing the right thing.
Center your heart in mine
and all will be well,
all will be right.

~

Suppose every time you opened your mouth to speak,
to say anything
from, "I have a headache,"
to, "So-and-So is a fool,"
to, "Good night,"
these words came out first,
"With God all things are possible."

If you could experience the truth of these words
in the depths of your heart,
your own words would be endowed with new vigor, clarity
    and courage.
The way you speak,

which reflects the way you think and go about your life,
does not have to be an old, worn path.
The point here is not to be "good,"
or merely to cultivate "positive" thinking,
or to pump yourself up to an attitude
that has no connection with everyday reality.
The point is to *become* thankfulness, expectancy, faithfulness,
to *become* eyes, ears and mouth
open to every kind
of God-given possibility.

Your small I am
must flow into the large *I AM.*
Do not fear,
go with love,
know you are helping
to create *me* anew
as you go.

Love

You are protected by the shield of love.

~

You must love yourself,
then all else will fall into place.

~

Give yourself more time, more space, more kindness.

~

(I said, "I'm sorry, you're going to have to take me as I am today.")

I do take you as you are —
always.
I'm not sure you take yourself as you are.

Those are little details, little nothings, you're focusing on
        now.
Let them go,
look for the larger.

Give thanks for your very own large, beautiful spirit.
The not-taking-yourself-as-you-are,
that is what you must give up.
Allow me to love you where you are.

~

Love your body.
Listen to it.
It is true in a way
you are not always able to be true
in the soul realm.
Respect its needs,
marvel at its wisdom and beauty,
be familiar with its shortcomings
without pampering it.

~

Every single choice you make produces ripples.
If the motive is true love,
love will come forth in others.

~

One soul with the right attitude of trust and love
can cast a light over all the earth.
Listen to your heart as it responds
to the light or the dark of each thought.

Ever and again
follow my light,
turn from the darkness
to love.

~

The heart that loves
and seeks the truth
both rests in heaven
and is willing to go through hell
for what it loves.

~

You can communicate truly only through me,
through love.
When you communicate through me
you are blended into the stream of the Godhead.
The difference between purely human communication
and communication through me
is like the difference between sun and battery power.
The battery runs on its own energy
and works for only so long.
It is not a false energy
but it has its limits.
When you are with me,
in me,
there are no limits.

If you love one particular dog,
you love all dogs,
you are tuned into all dogs,
you enhance all dogs.
There is this law of love wherein
you enter into the all
through love of the one.

You ask about talking with the angels.
That is as simple
as making time to talk with someone you love.

Send forth love through gladness for the other,
through tender concern and an attitude of constant hope,
not through mental willing.
The heart gives, the mind directs.
One creates the letter,
the other provides the envelope in which the letter is sent.

The way of love
does not talk about itself.
It gives,
cultivates patience and tolerance,

is kindness,
interest in all,
sweetness,
simple wholeness and practicality.
Transformation occurs
wherever this love is present,
it isn't "applied,"
simply *is*.

~

The inner work is *so* important.
Every single step and gesture
offered inwardly in the name of love matters.
It matters more than you can ever see.
You are pushing back the darkness a bit,
making way for the light.

~

You want to know more with your mind.
You want to know why you have to put up with this and that.
You should want, rather, to love more with your heart.
The only true meanings,
the only true seeing and knowing,
can be found in the heart.
So let your path be the path of love—
simple and direct.

~

Rilke was correct
when he said a whole constellation of things
have to go right
in order for people to love one another.
The angels are there to help—he knew that also.
Love is *my* work,
the constellations are lined up to help.

Imagine the slow, beautiful, precise motions of it all.
It can never be hurried,
it is slow not only in movement but in tone.
All that happens has been in the making
even before you were first born.
Bow down before the wisdom of it all,
let wonder flood your heart.
For your hand to take up this pen and to write these words—
that has taken more than you can possibly understand.
God laughs at your motions, your groping,
the same way you laugh with delight
at the first movements of a baby's fingers in the air.
God shaped these movements,
He is the master choreographer,
the master of your true will.
Nothing is without meaning.

You feel the majesty of it all.
Flow with it.
In meek amazement give thanks for the stars,

for the beings standing behind and within them.
The moon spills its bounty onto the earth,
for it is time.

If your earthly heart and mind can't keep up with what's coming,
don't panic, or give in to discouragement,
be glad for your ignorance.
The heart is being shaped anew,
while the earth is being born anew.

Amen.

～

(I asked if the marriage of dear friends could be saved and heard:)

O woman,
inspire man
out of the goodness, beauty and longing in your heart.

O man,
win the heart of woman
out of the strength, truth and longing in your heart.

O man and woman,
till you find one another anew,
the heart is broken,
the way unclear,
the night and day both dark.

～

Love the connections you have with *all* people—
near and far,
family and friends,
neighbors and colleagues.
Don't try to be free of these connections
even if they bring you no joy.

Enter the connections with my patience and compassion.
Not only do they help bring you into this world,
you can help bring them into my world.
How often have you longed for connection?
Look back through here (my journal),
the longing is everywhere!
Again and again you seek connection
with me,
the spirit,
those you love,
even with those you are yet to love.

You are not always conscious of this
but it is the essential gesture of your soul.
So, you must acknowledge connection also
with what you are connected with from the past,
especially with what hurts.
Don't dodge it.
There is no better way to move into the future,
my future,
into me.

(later)

If this (loving the connections) is hard,
ask yourself in the spirit of honesty,
"What would my life be like
if I had never known this person ?"

If, after that,
you still cannot find a shred of gratitude within yourself,
ask for God's mercy.

I hung on the cross
my heart fully exposed,
my connection to humanity laid bare.
So must your heart be exposed
at the right time,
in the right place,
if the new connection is to be born.

～

When you are angry at,
or irritated by,
this or that person —
bless that person!
Wish happiness, success, good health,
true spiritual unfoldment on that person.
This is easier and more effective than thinking,

"I've got to be grateful..."
Really, is there anyone
whom you do *not* want to see blessed?

~

You never lose those you love.
(Those who have died.)
They are within you,
you know that.

~

Something may be withheld from you
because you are seeking it for the wrong reason.
For example you may want messages from me for those dear
     to you,
to insure your usefulness or closeness to them.
This is a wrong reason.
I can speak to others through you
only when there is genuine, selfless love.
When your soul is lit with such love
you may not even be aware that I am speaking through you.

~

Fear can bring people together.
If it's the only way,
it will be used.
The better way is through listening and loving.

People can come into me,
the one and only sanctuary,
without knowing my name.
It is happening all the time.
When you know my name, however,
you can draw close to my heart
and work in full consciousness
throughout the earth and heavens.

Work to develop your heart center,
hold others in it, as if in a cradle.
Surround them with light.
You need not "know" about their troubles.
Believe in the power of the light in your heart.
It can hear and see,
can reach across great distances,
penetrate darkness,
dissolve sadness.

Keep to yourself what the spirit world tells you about others
until the moment comes when it may be shared.
In the end all is known, must be known.
Your knowing may be the deepest comfort to another soul
at the right moment,
the moment of true hunger.

When one knows and loves another soul,
it is food and sunshine for that soul.
Loneliness melts away before this knowing.
What is rough becomes smooth,
what is crooked is straightened.
This knowing is of the heart, not the mind.
It never seeks to own or control.

~

Marvel at the many forms of my love,
delight in them:
daughterly love,
sisterly love,
motherly love,
womanly love.
How people limit themselves today!
They limit love again and again to the body.
When you let love rise to become true gladness for life,
gladness that gives and asks for nothing in return,
it becomes a creative force,
a force that touches *everyone* with whom you come into contact.

Do not be afraid to love wholeheartedly.
You know what is right and wrong,
you know when your giving will be misunderstood,
trust this knowing.

~

Love me in all creatures,
in all plants,
in the sky, stars, clouds and sun.
Your love quickens *my* body,
helps it to merge with all.

～

When you give in to personal desire,
no matter how lofty, deep, great or pure it seems to you,
you lose something;
you lose access to me because you are closing me out.
There is an *immense* difference between love and desire.
You are coming closer to understanding it;
you will take big steps forward
when you learn to distinguish between them
and then choose in full consciousness.

You can move on as you wish
yet only to the degree you can relinquish your desires.
You know this.
The way is open.

～

Relinquish intimacy
and you will find vision.

～

Come into the sanctuary of my being.
I love *every* bit of *every* soul that loves me,
no matter how simple or complicated their way of loving.

~

True healing can only come through sacrifice.
True sacrifice can only be an act of love.

~

Sacrifice is the essence of love.
Until that is recognized
relationships will fail,
work will be drudgery,
children will have no compass by which to live.
Sacrifice your discouragement in work
and the true idea will rise up anew.
You have chosen your work
and must find
every way to make yourself worthy of it,
then fruits will come forth.
Every minute you can give up something
for another,
for an ideal.
Give up your sleepiness,
give up your physical discomfort,
your doubt, fear, and uncertainty,
offer up your unknowing

(knowing the difference between true and false unknowing),
give up your self pleasure.
Gratitude and sacrifice are two tools
indispensable on the frontier.

~

To love is to bring my light to shine on everyone you meet,
on all you look upon.

~

Your gift to the world
must be the continual listening and looking
for the spirit through love.
By doing this you are giving to the spirit
and are in turn
filled up, renewed, transformed.

~

You who feel so poor and impoverished,
give love—
give the little you have,
give and give,
that, through giving, you may discover
the well of living water in your heart.
Draw deep in faith
and love will overflow through you.

To those who give all, all is given.

Give love.
Seek truth.
As you give love
it will be given unto you.
As you seek truth
it will seek you out.

One calls forth light from you,
the other draws light to you.

Through love and truth
one is granted the power
to work directly on the hearts of others.
Both are necessary,
both are strengthened when this is done.

You may experience one
and then the other separately—
love, and then truth,
like the left, and then the right hand,
at the piano.

To learn to act with both,
that is the goal.
Now one carries the melody,
now the other,
now the two create it together.
If you look at the word through love and truth
and listen to it with love and truth,
you'll see and hear it objectively, but not dispassionately.
You'll see things for what they are
without being threatened by them,
without judging.
You'll know they're a part of you.

Love and truth require honesty, respect and openness.
Truth cannot be grasped all at once
no matter how large the knowing in the heart.
Love cannot be grasped all at once
no matter how present or clear the mind.

You can feel yourself
now closer to one,
now to the other.
Learn to distinguish between critical thoughts of others
and true discernment.
Learn to distinguish between personal sympathy
and true love.

~

Your devotion must find its own shape
from out of your heart,
rather than your mind imposing shape on it.

~

Don't let the dazzle of the mind obscure the heart.

~

As with animals
and all else in the natural world,
you must earn the trust of the spiritual world.
That is possible
through quiet, genuine, loving interest.

~

Let not your focus be on healing,
but on loving.
Until you know how to ask rightly in my name,
seek only to give love.

Is it possible to love every single person
for what that person is?
Yes!

In these times of muchness
the each is lost,
the inner sense of each and only is lost.
People scramble to feel worthy,
to have a title, to have self-esteem, confidence,
whatever you choose to call it.
Having lost their connection with the divine
they develop instead huge wants that suck inwards.
The divine must flow outwards, not inwards.
In order to heal in my name
one must be ready to be faceless, nameless.

Those who can enter into the eachness
anywhere, with anyone, any time
have no need of games and titles.
In each they find all.
They help to reconnect to the all.
This the longer more difficult route in healing,
but it is the truer way.

Don't be sidetracked by glamorous methods
no matter how much "sense" they make to you.

To know your own heart,
to find love in it,
to give love from it,
to see the world through it,
that is the task of healing.

All kinds of help will come to you
at the moment you love.
Loving is an activity,
not a method.

~

Have no wish nor want,
simply give.
As you give of your heart,
so is it filled up and transformed by me.

You can come to perceive this.
You *can* and *will* and *must!*
This giving has no boundaries,
it feeds the dead as well as the living,
it can move backwards in your "time"
and forwards into your "future."
Light of truth from without,
light of love from within:
you will travel back and forth between them
until the two become one stream.

The point where the physical and the spiritual meet,
where the meeting can be truly alive,
is in me, in my love.
I opened the door for the spiritual into the physical world
and for the physical into the spiritual world.

Q: How can we find this door?

You can't go through it for once and for all.
You must find it again and again
until *all* that is physical has been brought through to me:
then death will cease.

Q: Why can't one go through the door once and for all?

Because you contain not only the Earth
but *all others* within yourself.
When there is love in a deed, spirit is kindled;
when there is no love, spirit is slain.
You can find love only through me,
whether you know my name or not.
When there is true love for another,
for an idea, a group, a simple deed,
you are *kindling* love, *kindling* spirit.
You can love to the extent that you are open to me.
You can love one person and through that one,
love the whole world.
One genuine love,
no matter how small to human eyes,
can feed the cosmos.
When you grasp hold of love,
it moves into desire;
greed is kindled, not spirit.
Be fully sensitive to the tragedy
of love today being dragged down into greed.
That is death for the spirit.

Rest awhile.

(later)

There are many ways to view the spirit of love.
Recognize the powerlessness of human will to manipulate
     true love.
Thank God that is so!

You choose to love or not to love.
You choose to open or not to open.
I wait for you.
I never force myself on you.

The great sin is not to love,
to close entirely to it,
to turn away from it.

⁓

(These words came at the end of Advent:)
Give thanks
for the world that was created out of love
and for the love that now seeks to recreate itself
in you.
Be open,
that love may be born ever anew
in your heart.

Be glad,
that love may take root, grow
and shine out from you
to warm the world.

Be faithful
that love may use you
to link heaven and earth.

Sing O heart,
as you enter into the depths
and find therein
the brightness and glory
of your own being,
and your lord.
Sing!

The spiritual world stretches out
on every side
from the point that is you.
It is there in air,
in moonlight and sunlight,
in earth, wind, water,
in tree, stone, flower,
in every living creature.
It is there in the movements
of your mind and heart.

Thoughts are your limbs in this world,
feelings your muscles.
All work together, flow together.
The God-given will carries you forward
through its invisible,
all-encompassing lungs.
Breathing you in and out gently,
holding you forever
on this side and the other.
The hugeness of it all
can be threatening yourself,
but when you let go,
and allow my love to carry you,
you are made whole,
you are made one in all.

Ask

Those who ask are more dear to the divine
than those who know.

~

The true questions arise in the heart
as truly as do the true answers.
You cannot have one without the other.
How often are your questions so much clamoring of the
    earthly mind?
Allow your heart to arrive at and depart from
the true questions
without pressure from the earthly mind.

~

Some questions are demands,
others are expressions of openness.
When you ask from the point of power within yourself
you are given power.
What is this point of power?
It is where the connection with the highest in you,
the spirit within, occurs.

I die a bit when this power is abused.
I rise when it is used correctly.
I cannot interfere with your freedom to choose your way.
To ask out of love strengthens me,
makes for spiritual life.
To ask out of the smaller ego, takes from me.

~

Don't ask questions unless you mean them,
truly mean them from deep down.

~

Try to make your questions specific,
don't let them be big, general, vague wonderings
or that's what you'll get back.

~

You must *ask* and *take*.
Don't hesitate,
don't doubt what you heard—
Take!

Take light,
take faith,
take hope—
and move forward.

~

What is the most loving thing you can do
for this person (or situation)?
Ask yourself.

~

You're pushing too hard in your prayer life
for what *you* want to see in others.
Let go of that.
The spiritual world is so vast,
so immense in its possibilities,
do not block the way with your preferences.
Pray only for my light on and in others.
Leave the rest, the details, to me and to the angels.
Remember it is the intention that matters, that is all.
Even for yourself, leave the imaginings to me.
Let this teach you that true love brings freedom;
it is free of personal expectations,
it rejoices in the other,
that is all.

~

Sure, I could answer your questions one by one,
from question 1 to 2 to 3,
and so on.
Questions can be like a cancer when they loose touch
with the true intention within the heart.

~

Get yet more direct.

Q: How?

Don't just rededicate yourself to the direct approach,
dig in,
dig down to those questions,
the *big* ones.

Q: Which ones?

One can always go further,
deeper,
into the riddles of one's life.
There is no ending,
there is only becoming.
As you ask you will be transformed.

It is all so simple,
yet you make it so complicated.
The mind can elaborate endlessly,
can question, and doubt, and unsettle,
while the heart longs
to weave it all into the most wonderful pattern.
Not a simple pattern, mind you,
an intricate, glorious pattern
made up of pure, simple impulses.

Yes! I will answer every question you ask from your heart.

Listen

I not only take you into my heart,
I would have you listen to my heart.

~

As you hear
so are you awoken.

~

In patience, gentleness, and hope
the faithful soul
must wait and listen.

~

The greatest obstacle to inner hearing is,
"Why would Christ speak to me?
Why would he have anything to say to me?"
People have allowed themselves
to become so sunk in their bodies and minds
they see no way, or reason, to identify with me.
It may come across as false modesty.

Q: Are you speaking of skepticism?

No, skepticism can be healthy,
Thomas's skepticism was healthy.
Self-despair, self-hatred:
they are not openings.

~

Your gift to the world
must be the continual listening and looking for the spirit
    through love.
By doing this you are giving to the spirit
and are in turn
filled up, renewed and transformed.

~

Like it or not
you cannot love me, or listen to me,
without loving and listening to others.

~

It's all a matter of which voice you listen to.
Are you listening to the voices in your head
or to the voice in your heart?
Are you listening to the frightened solider,
the arrogant commander,
or the wise king?

~

You can listen to your scolding self
or to your forgiving self,
wherein I dwell.
You can listen to your limiting self
or to your expanding, singing self,
wherein I also dwell.
Come now, choose.
Don't hesitate, for with hesitation comes doubt.
Choose!
And move on.

~

Your impulse is to give away what is given to you
as soon as you receive it.
This is commendable in many ways
but you need to develop deeper listening.
This means holding what you hear within,
allowing it to take root.

Ease out all impulses to give or act immediately.
Prune back the blossoms that there may be more blossoms.

~

Only inner activity is going to get you out of
this state of nothingness,

inner listening,
then acting on what you believe you have heard.
Listen-act.
Listen-act.
There is no other way.
I will come to meet you to the degree you move towards me
as you listen.

~

I need a place to rest,
hearts that will listen and be there,
minds that are willing to put all thoughts aside,
except for the thought of me and my light.
That is why I ask again and again
if you are willing to listen,
to spend a lifetime listening.

~

When you're with others, listen for me,
both in what they say, how they look, and what you hear within.
Your ability to listen can *always* grow.
Let the intention to listen be your teacher and guide.

Enlarging your capacity to listen will, quite naturally,
guide you to the inner screen.
You have already experienced this many times
without being consciously aware of it.

Q: Am I just to "listen" or to "listen for certain things"?

Ah, now you're getting more specific. This is good.
It might be confusing to you, but it's good.
Listen for me—the *sound* of me.
There are many channels,
many voices speaking,
many forces competing for each person's attention.
You know when you're on my channel,
you know the "feel" of it.
You know when you're shifting from channel to channel aimlessly,
you know right off when you come near a channel you want
    no part of,
you move by its pull and go on.
When you tune into my channel
you find you *know* the answers to many questions
without even having to put them into words.

             ⌒

Always be listening,
always be giving
when you meet with others,
not just reflecting, reacting.
The small mind wants to be prepared,
wants to "shine,"
and be witty, clever, smart,
the center of it all.

This mind dreads awkwardness, uncertainty,
not having anything to say.
The heart that rests in me
is above these worries,
never fears emptiness or silence.

Stop every now and then
and ask yourself when with others,
"Are these words
coming from my mind or my heart?"
Learn to listen to yourself as you speak,
identify the source of your own words.
As you do this you will find
you are more able to hear
where others are speaking from.

~

When you listen to your friends speak about their worries,
do not just feel with them,
listen also for the heart's response to their words.
This means going beyond what you personally and immediately
agree or disagree with.
You may hear nothing at the moment,
but keep listening,
keep open.
An impression may arise in you later,
minutes, days, even weeks, later,

an impression that tells you how to help your friend,
through words, actions or prayer.
Trust it.
Act on it.

~

Feel the vibrational note of things deep down
stirring, shifting, moving.
As this note sounds in you
listen.
Listen for the earth,
and my body in the earth.
Attempt to attune to it.
For it speaks to the stars, the sun, and the moon,
even as you speak from your heart to those you love.

~

Many levels of messages can be received.
It's important to know the differences between them.
There are messages that come from outside time and space
dealing with the essence, the core of things.
There are messages that come from within time and space
which may not necessarily be specific.
They come to nudge you,
to offer encouragement,
even to warn or prepare you.

~

Today I will ask the questions
and you will bring me the answers.
Listen carefully.
Listen in every direction.

~

The human mind has made it possible for connections
to be made quickly, anytime, across vast distances
and yet the human soul is starved for contact, *real* contact.
Allow your spirit the space
in which to learn to make contact
with the true spirit of communion and community.
It is there,
it is waiting.

~

(I said I wished I, and others close to me, could hear exactly
what we are meant to do, day by day.)

But you can!
If you trust me,
listen carefully
and act on what you hear,
it will become easier and easier to see the way.
Why can't my words be the starting point,

the stimulus
for every action?
You say, "Yes, but am I not supposed to think for myself?"
As if listening to me
means turning your thinking off.
Or you say, "Yes, but I have to make a living"
as if listening to me isn't living.
Dear friends, the work you do with me can be as concrete
as laying bricks one by one.

~

There is the inner Word
and there are the outer words;
try to distinguish between them.

The inner Word
is that which speaks
in the highest in you,
in your I AM.
Its voice is faithful, hopeful, ever loving,
never blaming, criticizing, disparaging.
When you are attuned to this Word
you can hear it in others
near and far,
beyond all time,
and in the great worlds
above, below, and all around.

Through the inner Word
you come into yourself, your place, your way,
those with whom you are in accord.

The inner Word
truly heard and truly spoken
is in the heart of now and always.
It is the thumbprint of your spirit,
the core of your being,
the seed from which pure will unfolds.
It may not come to you as you expect,
in the same way you hear through your physical ears,
but it *is* there.
Listen for it
with joy and expectation.
Once found,
return to it gladly, daily,
to be renewed.

Q: Do you have to hear the Word within before you can hear
   it within others?

Do you have to love yourself
before you can love others?

Yes.

But how does a child
come to love itself
if not through the love
given to it by others?
There *are* exceptions
but always,
even there,
it is the love from God
which enables you to love yourself.
God withholds it from none,
bestows it on all.

It is the same with the Word.

Listen:
the Word sounds forevermore.
You choose to hear or not to hear it,
respond or not respond to it.
The more your heart opens to it,
the more you find it
both within and in others.

Never assume you hear it better than another.
How many wars have arisen out of this assumption?
Listen and judge none.
Listen and know you are loved.
Listen and love.

The inner Word
is too vast
for you to "have" it in one lifetime.
When you think with pride
that you "have" it,
it becomes mere outer words
devoid of power.
When it "has" you,
has your love, your trust, your faith, and full attention
you become vast,
bread for the world to feed upon.

Lift the Word to new heights,
it has sunk so low!
Become its servant.

Souls must watch their words,
must protect them,
earn them,
learn anew to love through them.
The Word has been stripped bare,
gnawed down to the bone,
over-dressed, dissected, made foolish.
The Word must be restored to its full power and dignity.

The Word is breath shaped into energy.
Energy that longs to move
straight from the heart of the Father
over all creation.

Yield to the Word in its power.
Let it move within
and flow out,
pure and clean.
Help to make it new
through your willingness, patience, and faith.

~

God's language is the language of praise,
of gladness, thanksgiving, wonder, and reverence.
My language is the language of love,
of adoration.

Learn to attune the inner ear to both,
to know their differences and similarities,
to know them as they move within your heart.

"Differences" does not mean
they are two separate, distinct languages,
for each nourishes
and helps to shape the other.
Yet, at the same time,

they are different in subtle ways.
Sensing the differences
will help your spirit,
and mine also,
to become more articulate.

How do you express praise?
How do you express love?
How can each be expressed
through your life
so you can learn to call upon the presence
of each, and both?
Dwell on these questions.

⁓

There is meaning!
Oh yes, dear heart,
as you listen within and without,
you will sense the meaning unfolding.
If you are open, reverent, prayerful, patient,
the meaning will unfold before you
like beautiful, woven fabric.
If you are doubtful, angry, impatient, fearful,
all is closed to you,
you become a rend in the fabric.

Those who remain open and glad
are a part of the weaving,
they create and recreate the earth.
By their very example
they create others.

Shine, dear heart.
Attempt to shine in the glory of your risen Lord.

Rejoice!
Rejoice in the knowledge
that my word can be heard in the heart
of every man and woman!
Where one is,
how old one is,
what language one speaks,
what one does,
what schooling one has had—
they make no difference.
All souls centered on me are One.

Listen to and work with the pain

Pain is a messenger,
acknowledge its presence
and listen to it
with an open mind
and a thankful heart
no matter how ugly or unfamiliar
its face may be.

~

You can't just will or pray pain away.
You must recognize it for what it is: it's a message.
A painless existence means a neutral, lightless existence.
So do not will someone else's pain away.
With each pain comes a promise of light.
Pain can crack one open.
Imagine rocks being cracked that light may enter.
Imagine jewels being found within these rocks.

Pain itself is never the problem.
Stubbornness, greed, blindness
they are the problems.

Give thanks for pain
that it may work its way into, through and out (of a soul)
rightly and quickly.

～

No learning without some pain.

～

Pain often arises out of an unwillingness to see the truth.

～

Let the pain of not feeling connected with me guide you,
don't fight it.
Let it guide you back to the true connection.
When there is true hunger, food is not far away.

Can you imagine this connection?
Imagine it being there for *everything* you do.
When you work it is there, guiding you.
When you play it is there, delighting in the freedom of
     your spirit.
When you are with others, it is there leading you to
     true listening,
making light available to other souls.
Can you imagine any higher work?
I am right here longing to work, play, listen, and love
     through you.

～

I am not asking you to be in pain.
I am inviting you to give me your pain.
How long you want to be in pain is *your* choice.
I am here to help.

～

There is something in you
that does not believe in the spiritual world.
Don't battle it,
that will polarize you inwardly,
work *with* it.
It is the earthly mind waiting
to be won over,
transformed,
raised up.

～

The denial is important.
Every soul that loves me
must go through the denial as Peter did.
For some it is short and easy,
for others it is long and grievous.
The sleep and the scattering:
they are important too.

~

If you can lovingly recognize the part of you that doesn't believe,
that causes you pain and confusion,
you'll be able to see it in others.
It is raw ore.

~

Patience, insight, joy and direction will be given to you
to the degree that you curb and transform
your impatience and loneliness.
Die to the longings and graspings of the mind.
Die and become.
Welcome a life in service to the fellowship of light.

~

Prayer is the exercising of the inner muscles,
the spiritual muscles
that hold you together
and help your spirit self to move
with strength, grace and power
through the world.

To truly pray for another
or for others,
means not to plead,
but to hold that person,
marriage, family, city or even country,

up to the light with gladness, hope and love
when they are unable to do it themselves.
And to continue to do this
no matter what the outer eyes see.

In the physical world
you are contained in a body and cannot share your muscles
with another
(except to lift or hold them outwardly).
It is different in the spiritual world;
there your spiritual "muscles" can enter right into another,
and can help to provide strength and structure
as long as you exercise thankfulness and openness to my light.

Your discovery of ways to pray,
meaning ways to enter more and more into gladness, hope
        and love,
will give you stronger and stronger spiritual muscles.
You don't just use one machine
in the exercise room,
you use different ones for different parts of the body.
Discover the largeness of the spiritual body.
Prayer should never be passive,
you don't exercise by lying on a mat on the floor wanting
        to be strong.

Prayer is *heart* activity.
Learn by doing,

if only at first through small, uncertain movements
towards gladness, hope, and love.
You will learn about depression in others
and how to deal with it
to the degree that you can bring yourself to me.
Depression is a cloud over the spirit.
One forgets what it is like to be in the sunshine
of gratitude, hopefulness, and sweet connection.
Help the memory to stir in others,
for it is in all souls.
When the memory is awakened,
the journey begins,
the hunger is too great to be ignored.

No matter where one is,
no matter what the situation
or the outer needs,
the memory *can* stir.
A reflection of long ago,
time in the Garden,
sweetness of love,
real love.

Cultivate hopefulness
that the way back be revealed.
It will then become the way forward
through catastrophes and upheaval
both individual and universal.

To each one who suffers from depression:
You are a child of God
no matter your age or experience.
Remember that!
Remember and know how joyfully
He awaits your return.

~

Ask yourself in those moments
when you long to help or heal another,
"Will this provide temporary relief
of soul and bodily pain,
or will it help this soul
to find true power and wisdom
within itself?"

~

In order to help others
you must be entirely free of the need to feel needed,
of the need to give advice
or feel important.

~

(I had asked that a certain person be spared pain.)

Would you have me remove the test she, herself, asked for?

Give thanks,
deep thanks,
for the infirmities,
the afflictions,
the aberrations,
the doubts and fears
of those you love.
Give thanks silently in your heart
and those souls will be helped.

~

Learn to take others into your heart in gladness,
without weariness or sadness.
I will teach you this.
I need you unencumbered.

~

Every pain,
every joy
can lift up
or pull down.
You have it in your power to decide
which way it will go,
where it will go.

Deciding to lift up,
to give all over to me,
brings new life to all in heaven.

Be not ashamed if you are pulled down.
Be humbled,
be still,
know I am still here,
still waiting,
know you can choose again.

Praise God!
Praise God!
And again praise God for what you are given
through pain and joy.
For when they are given to me
wings sprout,
new paths unfold,
flowers burst into blossom,
and ripen into fruit.
The music from your soul pours forth
in living streams and colors.

Amen

Forgive

All the words that are given to you
may sound beautiful
and may move you deeply
but they mean *nothing* at all
if you do not know how to forgive.
Forgiveness does not mean attempting to be tolerant
of the failings or shortcomings
of others, or of yourself.
Forgiveness does not wear a half smile.
Forgiveness is the complete, glad, ready relinquishment
of your perception of and feelings about the matter at hand.
When you forgive
you are making room
for the love that waits to be poured
into you and the other.
When you forgive
you are clearing the way for the Word
to sound forth and be heard.

To let go and forgive
doesn't mean becoming weak and wishy-washy;
it means moving into new strength,
new inner assurance, new faith.

~

For the living to forgive the dead—
That is like moving mountains!

~

There will *always* be strands of doubt in you.
Rather than trying to finger through to their source
and pull them out,
weave in new strands of light, faith, hope
and, through them all,
forgiveness.

~

There is no excuse for not acting from your highest.
Don't say, "I am only human…"
There is only forgiveness.
The sooner you ask for it and move on,
the better.

Look

Remember always to look for the good,
to look for what you, in your heart, are *for*,
rather than spending time thinking about
what you are against.
Heart thought must lead mind thought
into the way of the good, the true, and the beautiful.

This ability to turn to the light
must become so natural, so instantaneous
that darkness is shed quickly, dropped, passed by . . .

If you focus on what you don't want, you encourage it.
If you focus on what bothers you, you encourage it.
Focus on the good, on what you love, on what you admire in
    others
and those things will grow
both in others and in you.
This does not mean being blind to darkness.
Quite the contrary.
As you invite me to come closer

my compassion will help open your eyes
to both the light and the dark.

Focus on my light.
Seek it.
Seek to become familiar with it,
to be in its presence,
to be enlightened by it.
There is not only my light,
there is also a false light.
Darkness imitates everything.

Q: How can I distinguish between them?

As with my voice,
your heart vibrates to my light, the true light.
The true light enables your heart to sing, to be steady, to know.
Your heart *knows* the eternal, the best and highest in others,
it *knows* the voice of goodness,
it *sees* goodness.
The voice of the shadows suggest limitation,
pulls down, picks apart, questions, doubts.

Ask from your heart for my light.
Ask that it show you the way,
fill you with courage, certainty, and love.

Ask,
that through the asking
your hearing and seeing may be strengthened.

~

Become a disciple of the *I am*.
Greet every person you see inwardly with,
"You are spirit.
You are beautiful.
The *I am* is in you."

~

Look and listen—
Rouse yourself to go at once *beyond* yourself
(your worries, fears and doubts)
and to enter truly *into* yourself, into your center,
wherein is the spirit, the *I am*.

~

There is an inner screen on which you can see
whom you are to pray about or talk with.
Seek to open this screen.
It is the same screen on which dreams appear.
Get the feel of it.
Any time of day,
stop and feel for it.
Be open and grateful for whatever you get.

Later you will be able to tune into what your heart seeks
and *knows* it must connect with.
Inner vision can travel anywhere,
backwards, forwards,
throughout the world,
into the heavens.

Looking to me and being guided by me;
doing that does not automatically mean
you are free of human feelings.
When powerful feelings rise up
and you think you've lost me,
it may be that your vision of me
is being obscured by those feelings.

You feel threatened by certain thoughts,
look not to your security,
look to the true thought
and therein you will find security.
In mid-air your feet will find firm ground.

How to look for the true thought?
It is in love,
in me.
It *lives*
it *is*.

It will not be pinned to a name,
yet its words can be sharp as a knife
that cuts away the dead,
and all the forces that drag down.
It is fluid, supple, quick to bend
and quick to raise up.

You walk between the formless and the formed,
both call you forward,
one has a face, the other none.
Yet they are the same.
Only in movement can you know them,
only in movement can they use you.
Still the question—
experience it.
If there must be a question,
ask to be *in* it.

When in it
you are given exactly what the world needs.
Not a word too much,
nor too little.
Hunger is satisfied,
but not dulled.

Come unto me
know life and love in me.

Amen
and again, Amen.

If you want to meet the Holy Spirit,
be ready and willing to look upon all kinds of spirits,
dark as well as light.
Only when seen in this context
can the true and Holy Spirit shine forth.
Look with my eyes.
Be fearless
no matter what you see.

Seek the light,
      see the light,
            work with the light

Seek my reflection
wherever you are
in the words, lives, and souls of others.
Let it warm, inspire, and gladden you,
even as the moon reflects
the sun's holy light.
So may you live into a sense
of the many phases of my being,
then—now—always.

Seek the "new" news,
discard the "old" news:
all that cripples and paralyzes the highest in you.
You read the "new" news last Sunday (during prayer time),
it is still there, still new.
The spiritual world is not static.
Goodness, truth and beauty have movements and music
you've barely begun to imagine.
Find them, read them, tune into them,
let them shape you anew.

Learn to perceive through gratitude, through love and reverence,
learn to perceive with the eyes of the spirit,
and to hear with the ears of the spirit,
for the spirit world waits and longs to connect with you.
Learn to perceive the light and dark forces.
Learn that focusing on the dark, though sometimes necessary,
can actually encourage the dark.
Learn to take hold of the light
and to let the light take hold of you.
For the light will bring you direction, ideas to follow,
paths to tread.

My light is striving to come into being in you and in all.
It has no definite physical name or shape,
but it is not formless.
Bring your soul forward in gratitude, love and reverence
to meet my light,
and we shall find the new way together.

A. cannot see with clairvoyance
yet he *can* see through the reverence in his heart.
His reverence is an organ of perception,
it is there whether he knows it or not.
So it can be with all of you.
To strengthen your hearing,

and your sense of purpose and direction,
give shape to reverence.

This means having respect for every living thing—
you revere the spirit in it,
you greet it
even if you cannot see it.
Think on this.

You feel dismay over the past—
what does all that matter
if you are connected
to the light,
to reverence?

It does not matter.
If you are in the light
everything you do
(conscious or otherwise)
is permeated by light.
Nothing else matters.

What you think of yourself doesn't matter
if you are in the light.
If you are not in the light
your thoughts can become destructive.
The greatest work of art you can create
is yourself
as a vessel of the light.

Keep focused on the light
in simple, sweet devotion.

All the angels *are* in place,
all the help that is needed *is* there.
Believe!
Some day you will see
what you believe.

When you believe and have faith in these things
the light in you shines clear and steady.
You know the light as warmth,
now know it also as truth.
Know that the light can pass right through all feeling,
to your center, your spirit.
You will find a deeper, truer joy
if you come to know the light as truth.
Grow beyond your very own feelings.
This does not mean
ignoring them
or turning from them.
Grow through and beyond them
into my light which shines on all.
Be firm in the light of the highest truth,
that love may be born anew.

~

You can only take the light of truth
a bit at a time;
it would shatter you if it came as you want.
Trust that the heavenly beings
know how much you can take and when.
Trust their wisdom.
Do not ask what you are not ready for.

~

My light doesn't merely shine into and through you.
It must be taken in by your spirit,
eaten and digested,
then it can go forth.

Q: Must I become conscious of this activity for it to happen
and be effective?

It is always happening to some degree.
By rising above pain and being glad for it
people learn to shed light.
By opening to joy they shed light.
Also by opening to wonder and reverence.
The more conscious of these activities you are, the better.
In consciousness you can meet and work with me.
As my light comes closer, darkness is thrown into disarray.
Let awareness of this strengthen your resolve.

Every loving light-filled thought you send out to others
is as important
as every loving, generous action you perform.

Focus not on the self and its limitations
but on the divine.

You must develop trust
that you will know immediately when my light is there
and I am speaking.

You're trying to race ahead in your understanding.
Calm down!
Slow down!
Every step is important, every step matters.
You recognize already the true light comes from the heart area
and flows through and out to others from there,
even as blood is sent through your body.
Send light to others,
to those, both on this side and the other,
whose faces rise up in you.

Dwell in this activity in deepest reverence and wonder.
Understanding will come to you through the reverence and
the wonder.
There is no other way you can come to know those on the
other side.
Breathe in the love they send you in return.

~

As my light enters you,
and you pass it on,
it isn't used up.
Quite the opposite.
More light is generated.

~

Put up a shield of light around all you love to protect them.
Send light to their minds that they may be uplifted.
Send light to their hearts that they may be comforted,
warmed and centered in me.
Do not attempt to understand the how's and whys of it.
Do it.

~

See others with my eyes.
See me in others.
Let the two seeings become one.
That place where they meet is holy.

Healing can occur there.
Your inner and outer merge there.

～

Love through your eyes
if that comes more easily than through words.

～

Recognize that the true light comes from your heart
and flows through and out to others from there,
even as blood is sent through your body.

Send this light to others,
to those on this side and the other,
whose faces rise up in you.

Dwell in this activity in deepest reverence and wonder.
Understanding will come to you through the reverence and
  wonder.

～

Satan would take what is dearest to you,
would turn it into a weapon to keep you from the light.
If you can see through this and remain
faithful to the light,
in all simplicity and humility,
what is dearest to you will be given to you anew.

Rouse yourself ever and again
to ask for light,
for bread, water, and the way.
As you do this
and it is given to you,
so will you grow into me—
the only safe place.

~

Every light creates shadows.
The greater the light,
the deeper the shadows.
Let this be cause for thankfulness
not dismay.

~

Be aware of the darkness and shadows in others
but don't dwell on them.
Allow my light to carry you on and on—

~

There are false angels of light.
You can distinguish between the true and false angels
by way of the still, quiet center within.
Stand there in my name.
As my light approaches

the false light can be thrown into confusion and disarray.
This is happening more and more as I draw ever closer to
    humanity.

The only way you can hold close to me is through the cultivation
of being willing to admit you don't know,
of being willing to turn from your mental "knowing"
to openness to the unexpected and unknown.
Let me flow into you;
let this become an activity of the heart,
an openness, a listening, a giving of the heart.
You are ever new, ever young,
ever filled with joy, strength and clarity
when my light is working through you.

~

As you come to know me
you enter also into the sphere
of the corresponding opposite thought of me.
This is inevitable.

The realm of the Anti Christ opens up.
All that is the opposite of what I am comes forward too.
This must be.
Only by meeting,
and standing firm in the truth of what I am
are you able to turn away from what I am not.

That you can acknowledge
that you sometimes feel "fake" is good.
Just don't allow the feeling to dominate.
Rise up to the thought behind it
and see it for what it is:
the opposite of all that is real and good
in me and in my name.

The opposite of all I am
must be perceived for what it is,
then it can be transformed.

Evil and darkness serve their purpose:
to strengthen the good and the light.
Once you recognize this
and are able to apply the consciousness it brings
you will not only be able to see situations, moods,
and other people's paths for what they are,
you will be able to draw always on the true, on *me*, instantly
    no matter where you are,
whether in light or darkness.

⁓

To attempt to see and hear where others can't yet see or hear,
that is to begin to let my spirit live into the world.
Seek ever new ways of hearing,
of looking at things,
of being surprised and delighted anew daily
by the abundance of my spirit.

Let that come,
let that carry you.

~

Your inner picture of me
as the bearer of light and love
must grow so strong
that it is with you everywhere,
flowing from you into all,
washing over the dark pictures that surround your world.

You create this picture of triumphant love and light,
it cannot be given to you ready made.
As you work on it you transform yourself.
Great soul energy is required.
As you do this work
communication with others on the same path will open up.
So will the light from your created picture
penetrate into the problems of others around you.

Go beyond mere imagination,
do not just create a pretty, satisfying picture.
Put your heart into this task,
ask, "Light and love draw near,
come to my aid."

~

Learn to speak and act from your inner light reality,
rather than speaking and acting as things bother or please you.
See through the inner light, my light.

~

I am the light.
I am the one true reality.
When you sense my light
and move towards it's truth
all your separate, conflicting realities
fall away
and you begin to see things
as they are meant to be seen.
Then there is no question of who is right
and who is wrong,
as so often tears you all apart.

You experience not only the stages to becoming,
but the seed out of which becoming unfolds.
The need to be right, to own, falls away
so you can flow with the becoming.
I am the light.
Become like the unfolding seed
pushing up through the dark earth
towards the sun.
It doesn't push at the stones in its way,
it grows around them,
and presses on steadily.

Send down your roots in faith and trust,
reach up in hope.
Do not settle for anything less
than the full unfolding into fruit
of your own light-filled being.

Trust that my light is in you
leading you through the world,
like a flashlight
stretching ahead through the darkness,
exactly as far as you need to see,
resting on this or that person,
leading to this or that place,
revealing all you need to know.

Your eye—your inner eye—can flow with this light,
it can reach ahead and sense the terrain
before you've come to it.
It can warn you,
can send love before to pave the way.
So do not look aside,
do not be paralyzed by the darkness,
be fully confident,
for I am the light of the world,
I am with you.

I am the light of the world.

Feel how my light comes right down,
reaches back up,
rays out in every direction
through every part of your being.
You sensed it yesterday.
Use it.

Reach up
and open continually
beyond your personal feelings,
beyond your precious personal thoughts—
do not slight or ignore them
for that makes them stick to you all the more firmly.
Simply with courage and determination,
look beyond them
into my light.
Draw down all I am
into your mind, your eye,
your breath, your heart,
your stomach, the base of your spine.

Know my light to be warm
as well as bright.

Welcome the holy fire
without any fear of being burned away.
Let darkness be consumed,
let it be transformed into shining armor,
steady gladness,
selfless service.

~

Prayer is not just thinking the name of another person
or thinking what you think about that person
("She is sad"..."He needs help").
It is *seeing* that person as a divine and lovable being.
I will show you that way of seeing.
The work now is to *see* in prayer.

~

What do you know, in your deepest heart, needs doing?
Pay attention to that.
Enable it to become more and more clear to your inner eye
as you do it.
It's through the doing that it often comes into sight.

~

When you can find me
right where you are,
both inwardly and outwardly,

both in joy and sorrow,
clarity and confusion,
my light will,
like the sun,
rise and rise.
See it rising
in the faces of those you love.
See it rising all around
even when all looks dark.

For I am in your world.
I am everywhere you choose to be.
I am in your public and private moments,
your ins and outs
your waking and your sleeping.
Dear hearts, allow my light to grow ever brighter.
Allow it to rise up from below to hold you,
allow it to ray out from above to guide you,
allow it to surround and protect you.

Breathe deep

Breathe deeper and deeper.
Breathe right into the I am
and you will become surer, steadier.

⁓

Give thought to the in-breathing and out-breathing
of each day.
Breathe in my word,
breathe out praise and gladness.

⁓

Breathe in the particular,
breathe out into the universal,
breathe in the oneness in one,
breathe out into the allness of all.

⁓

Breathe in the light of truth.
breathe out the light of love.
Truth from without,
love from within.

Travel back and forth between them
until the two become one stream,
one complete breath.

⁓

Concentrate on the space in deep breathing
between the in and out breaths.
Learn to expand this space,
to dwell in it;
it is where the screen is.
In this space you can find my light
and direct it to others.

⁓

Learn to be aware of your whole body.
Close your eyes,
center your attention on your heart area.
It is the television screen.
How can you know if your attention is centered there?
One way is through consciousness of your breathing.
Lungs and heart are closely related, as you will discover.
Another way is through the inflow of light as your heart opens.
You not only feel its warmth,
you can come to see it inwardly.
The screen grows brighter and brighter.
Your hands and feet are satellite dishes.
Use them.

Palms up, to the heavens.
Feet down, to the earth.
(As you come to know the different centers in your body
you will come to know the earth.
The earth will speak to you.)
Your mind is the remote control.
Do not allow it to jump from channel to channel,
it is there to hold your attention to the screen.

Silently breathe out the words: O Lord My God.
Let these words come from your heart.
Let them soar on the out breath.
If it helps, imagine your heart as opening flower, gliding bird,
flowing water, shining star,
whatever it longs to become.

Silently breathe in the words: I am here.

Do not just think the words,
feel them.
Let them become a wish, an invitation.

Breathe out: O Lord my God.
Breathe in: I am here.

Feel your breathing growing deeper, steadier.
Watch the screen and listen.

Welcome thoughts,
ponder and live with them

The earnest, heartfelt wish to serve humanity
is far more important today
than having spiritual experiences
or longing for them.
True vision
will arise from out of this wish.

~

Your world is as large or as small as your thoughts.
Entertain large thoughts
and your world will become large.
Entertain small thoughts
and your world will shrink.

~

You must travel with me
because there are innumerable forces out there
that would and could lead you astray.
Imagine getting lost in the earth
or in the heavens.
Imagine that.
It *does* happen.

Don't just rest in a sense of fullness, of having,
when thoughts come to you.
Act on them, nourish them, share them.

~

You're going at it backwards today.
You're trying to eliminate everything in order to come closer to
        me
and what I have to tell you.
Don't eliminate,
don't block out,
take in all that is around,
everyone, everything, every problem.
Look for me in them,
then you'll hear me.

~

Through your reaching for me
you feed others,
even as others feed you
as they reach for me.

~

To take the thoughts you are given,
to work upon them inwardly
with vigor and dedication

till they are as real
as anything you do on the physical plane,
till they *become* the outer plane,
there is no higher work.

~

To foresee is to see that this and this will probably lead to that.
You have, however, the freedom to do this or this to get to that.
What do you want to cook for supper?
You can determine that,
pick the recipe,
change it,
or do without and make it all up.
Whatever you do, the outcome is quite possibly a meal.

There are thousands of recipes
simmering all around in different pots:
workshops, meditations, therapies, exercises ...
When you invite me in
I tell you my recipe
for each thing that comes to meet you.
As you've noticed
it sounds pretty much the same every day:
empty yourself,
listen,
act on what you hear.
The ingredients (which you provide) remain the same:

gratitude, honesty, faith,
and the willingness to go anywhere in the name of love,
even if the result isn't what you expected.
Sure, the pots get burned occasionally.

There are things that *are* foreordained.
There are things that *will* happen
as surely as your Father made you with the need to eat supper.
Your physical death is foreordained.
I cannot begin to tell you how hard it is
for those who meddle there.

~

Part of the task of coming into consciousness
is recognizing how imperative it is
that it be true consciousness of me,
not any form of fantasy.

Q: How can I know if I have a true consciousness of you?

It's a matter of the heart, not the head.
You can strive with your head to create pictures
and can convince yourself you are in these pictures
and they are real,
when in truth you are entirely off the mark.
This is the danger of certain exercise and meditations.
True consciousness lies in being able to start fresh every time

asking out of real need and devotion.
Those are your markers.
You know in your heart
when you're at the bottom,
when you're lost and starved.
Real need cannot be set up,
cannot be pretended by the honest heart.
The same goes for devotion.
Your heart *knows* the difference between sentimental piety
and true adoration.

⁓

I absorb into myself the effects of all wrong deeds in the world.
This doesn't mean you can sit back and rest easy.

Quite the contrary,
if you are the least bit alive to me
you will seek to change yourself,
to reshape that in yourself
which caused the wrong
and has the potential to do so again.
To come into me
is to descend into yourself as well.

There is no such thing as creating out of nothing.
God created out of Himself,
and needs you to create Himself further out of yourselves.
When this fails to happen there is a build up of forces
that can't flow and express themselves.
Wars and disasters can help set things in motion again.

Nothing can manifest outwardly
until you are so sure,
so anchored in the inner,
through what you see in the inner,
that you know the outer
to be but a shadow of the real.

There's that in you which wants to do the next thing.
This has nothing to do with ambition or the daily round of duties
you have placed yourself in.
It has to do with divine will.
It is good and wise.
Listen for it even though what it has to say
may only be about the daily round of duties.
Follow it.
It will make your actions cleaner, truer.

Your ideas—the ideas which seek to express themselves in
     your life—
are closely linked to your gifts.
They are the currency you are given to work with in this life.
Use them, spend them, give them to others
and more will be given to you.
Use them gladly, joyfully, without thought of return.
Do not hold onto them, hoard them, or believe they are yours
     alone.

Different ideas seek out different souls.
There are many ideas you are continually expressing to the world
that you are not aware of.
Self-awareness (self-knowledge) can help you to identify them,
make your life come into sharper, clearer focus,
can make the work (both in the world and upon yourself)
     more exact.
Impatience arises when you lose your connection
with the essence of the ideas that seek expression through you.
You lose the connection when your focus is too much on the outer.

Q: If I lose my connection with the essence of an idea, does
     the idea dry up and shrivel away?

An idea can continue to stand by a person for many lifetimes
waiting to be expressed.

The idea may be far more faithful to you than you may be to it.
Yes, ideas can shrivel up and die away but they usually wait.
One lifetime is nothing beside an eternal idea.
Ask yourself, "What is the ground work of my being?
What are the ideas I long to express?"
You will begin to see your life as the canvas
on which your highest self seeks to express certain ideas.
The more your higher self opens to my light,
the more lively the work becomes.
Recognize that doing "a lot" outwardly in the world
does not necessarily mean a person is filled with the higher.
Much work can go on in the depths, hidden from outer eyes,
for ideas work on many levels.
Many solitary souls work to make humankind more receptive
    to ideas,
they offer up their very physical bodies
that ideas may dwell on the earth,
they are light-houses for ideas that seek form here.

Judge no one,
you do not know what ideas people have come to express.
By loving all you are welcoming the highest in them.
Don't flounder around looking for ideas.
Let me be your central idea and from me will flow
all the ideas you
in your very individual makeup, need.

Even as you love an assignment, a set task, so can the work in
the higher realms become precise work, assignments if you want
to call it that.
Yes, you can find exactly what you must do next.
You must love and trust yourself, the highest in yourself, as
    well as me.
Let us go hand in hand.
Let us walk together
For I am with you.

~

It is possible for the birth of a higher being
to occur in a human being
at any point during that being's life on earth, at any age.
I am speaking of more than the birth of the higher self.
The higher self is awakened, yes,
and can then become a highway, so to speak, for other beings.
I am not speaking of channeling or possession.
I am speaking of a process that must, with time,
come to be fully conscious if it is to be effective.

To be fully aware of and alive to me
dwelling in you—
that is what must happen.
That is the only true route to freedom.

The parts must represent the whole.
There is a time coming when each soul
needs to move from itself to the whole.
It has nothing to do with sameness,
it has to do with unity,
with human hearts being united in me.

There has been a fellowship of light since all times.
It must expand on earth.
Try thinking of others before yourself.
When you are dragged down by sad or depressing thoughts
think of others whom you love
and the fellowship of light will come to your aid.
You are not alone,
are never alone.
Move from the one (yourself) to the *all,*
to the God-heart.

No matter how small the amount of time and attention
you offer to the spiritual world,
it is taken gladly, gratefully.
And something is *always* given in return.
You are not only raising up your being to the light when you
    do this,
you are raising up all of humanity.

You need your mind to say "No!"
to this or that thought or feeling.
You need your mind as the captain of your army,
the army of your being, both body and soul.
Connect with your captain,
give him orders and see that the army obeys these orders.
The army won't have faith in a captain who has no control
    over himself.
If he has control over himself he passes this control on to the army.
But remember, the captain is not the supreme commander,
the king is.
The king—
the voice of the highest—
within your heart.

You can invite a thought in
and you can ask it to leave.
You can take it in and let it shape
all that you do.
You can also take it by the neck
and throw it out
if it isn't congenial!

Be generous.
Be ever hospitable.

But stay alert.
Beware of the thoughts that force entrance
or sneak in when you're looking the other way.

~

"Success" as you think you want it,
and as you are now defining it,
is irrelevant.
The important thing is broadcasting light and love.
The spiritual world isn't measured in terms of success or failure,
the way you measure writing as successful or unsuccessful
because it is or isn't published.
The spiritual world is more fluid than that.
It's more fun too!

~

You can reach out in the spiritual world and touch anyone
    instantly.
This touching is of the utmost importance
although your eyes see nothing.
Do not judge by your eyes.
There is no quicker way to defeat or discourage yourself
than to judge by your physical eyes.
Learn to "pray without ceasing."
To pray without ceasing is to send forth light and love
    without ceasing.

People often mistake their outer physical work with their identity.
The outer work alone does not identify the person,
it is the inner, out of which the outer must arise,
that contains your true identity.
Can you imagine how your innermost suffers
when it cannot express itself outwardly?
Many today become dulled to this pain
as they get caught up in outer roles
that have nothing to do with the core of their being.
Some become physically ill
because their innermost cannot find outer expression.
Those who know their true work have nothing to fear,
all their material and spiritual needs will be provided for.
One should not be afraid to be "nobody" while seeking one's work.

People want me to be a corporation, an organization, a name,
something they can get hold of, join, identify with, et cetera.
I am in *all,*
in the oneness of all.
To be for me
if to find me in all,
no matter where or how they look.
To work for me
means to do without the title,
without the mission statement,

without an obvious outer salary.
It means to be homeless in the world
and yet to carry me in your heart everywhere.
My workers must be lights,
lights in the darkness.

~

It's fine to be business-like
but I don't want just a "business" relationship
with souls on earth.
I want a "love" relationship,
in which human hearts *and* minds vibrate to the highest
in everything they do.

~

Humans today want great truths in the form of information.
They want it neat and easy,
microwaveable,
better yet, something they can frame and put on the
     bedside table.
Change in *attitude* is the greatest work in these times.
There's an effort in this direction in many walks of life,
but still, people want it easy,
and fast.
Truth must work all the way through the soul into the physical,
no fancy bedside frame can catch this,
some pictures may have to be cracked before they're complete.

The elements reflect the intensity of what is to come.
Earthquake, flood, hurricane, tornado—
all are but outer whisps on the edge of inner movement.
Keep your eye on the light within
for the sake of your earth
as well as yourself.

Q: What is the weapon?

Keep your eye on the light,
be not afraid of the silence.
Look for the good in all.
Look beyond the darkness
calmly, with humor, and faith in the beyond.
A mighty shield of light surrounds those who look beyond.
Like the mask of a welder
this shield fits down over and around the true followers.
Be fearless in your looking beyond.

The second coming is larger than anything you can imagine.
It won't occur in the ways people expect;
it may not have much to do with those who profess themselves
to be "spiritually" oriented.

Humility—the ability to empty oneself again and again
of all preconceptions and set expectations
is extremely important
if one is to participate rightly in this event.
Empty yourself daily,
let your only thought be:
"I am here, Lord..."

~

The desire to know
and the hunger for intimacy with me
are two quite different things
yet both spring from the same spirit within.
Distinguish between them,
they are the need to see and to be seen,
objective and subjective aspects of being.
The human soul needs both
to enter into its divine inheritance.

As you find them,
open to them in me,
in my heart,
that it become activity in your heart,
and gift of your being
to each person you come into contact with.

~

You have to prepare and provide the mold
into which the will can be poured.

Q: How?

There is the initiation of the plus
and the initiation of the minus.
Most go for the plus.
In reality the way to me today
is through the minus.
It involves sacrifice.

Plus is asking for power,
minus is deliberately renouncing power.
It involves deepening the heart,
entering into the I am.

How do you sell the thought
that you are to give up all?
It's completely contrary to what the world urges today.
The only way to sell it is by doing it,
speaking through actions,
even through gestures and mere looks.
As you seek me
so do I seek others through you.

~

You—as a human being—are the meeting place
of the earthly and the divine.
Sometimes you feel the weight of one (the earthly).
Other times you feel the lightness and brilliance
of the other (the divine).
Let them blend together and create bread for the world.
Welcome both.
Don't fear either.
Have faith that I
can move through both
and can work in and through you.
Every human being, whether she knows it or not,
can be a vehicle of my work.

⁓

Pray for the world,
your beautiful world,
so small and yet so big,
so fragile and yet so strong.

Q: How?

See it.
See the shining orb.
See how the darkness accentuates the light.
See how the spinning accentuates the stillness.
No heart can say it all,

until all hearts say it,
sing it in its turning.
You are as small and yet as big,
as fragile and yet as strong
as this world
in which you live
and have yet to learn how to love.
I am with you.

Amen

(Several days later:)

Now picture the inner most being
of those you love
as you pictured your world:
shining, turning,
balancing darkness and light,
fragility and strength,
the small and the large.
Each being a seed of possibilities,
continuously going forth from and returning
into itself.

Bless those you love,
one by one
in their going forth.
That they, you, and all
may flourish.

Again, Amen.

⁓

The spiritual world does not progress in a straight line.
Events don't occur in A, B, C order.
Think of the water in the river
swirling,
folding back over itself,
working its way onwards in patterns.
Movements rise up from within and are created as well
by the river banks or objects in the water.
Seek to flow with me,
with my love,
with the *All*.
Be not afraid,
for fear can break the flow or block it.
Later you'll see the pattern,
you'll see how the spirit in you knew all along
where it was going.

⁓

Become these words:
gladness and joy,
that I may work through you more and more.

⁓

The mission of Jesus was to teach.
The mission of Christ is to shine (and bring light to all).

I am pure spirit, pure idea, pure light.
I do not have a physical body
yet I can penetrate and renew all that is physical.

There are other worlds
out beyond your earth.
Earth consciousness is coming closer
to entering into these worlds.
A cosmic shift is occurring.
For the earth to move with this shift
human consciousness must open to me.

Prepare yourself for the dream,
the dream that seeks to awaken in you,
linking heaven and earth.

The path comes into being by being tread upon,
by being discovered step by step.
Do not sit back and expect the path to appear of itself.
Move to find it,
even if the movement only means working toward a right attitude.
The inner compass can direct one in the right direction
so outer movement is not senseless wandering.

The spiritual senses are not opened all at once,
one must work to open them.
This work can be directed by the inner compass.
Where is this compass?
It is in your heart,
it is created out of faith.

The dead and the living need each other

The dead and the living need one another
as day needs night and night needs day.
Beyond all comings and goings,
the dead and the living are one.
Both must work together for the whole of humanity,
your Earth cannot exist without this.
When those in heaven and those on earth are brought together
in my name and my light,
real work can be done.

~

The dead have much to say
before they are reborn.
They need to be able to come and find their words
like tools waiting for them,
waiting to be put to immediate use.

Invite the dead to speak,
in my name invite, and welcome them,
my light will protect you.

Many on the other side cannot see me
and this is a source of pain and confusion.
Those on this side who are alive to me can help
by letting my light shine through their actions, words and
    thoughts.
(In this way) those on the other side
will be helped in their right work.

Q: How are you experienced on the other side?

I am experienced in the atmosphere,
as rarefied air,
as warmth and light,
as a quickening.

Q: Can you be seen?

Yes, but with a seeing different from the physical seeing
you use on earth.
I am seen from within.
I am seen through feelings, through love.

Q: With form?

Form as color,
as sound.

I fill all space.
Through me those who have died
can come to you
in the right way,
can communicate with you,
and you with them.
I am the road on which they come to you.

~

What you call a birth in the physical world
of a human being, or an idea
is, in the spiritual world, a death.
Ideas die into words,
thoughts die into deeds,
feelings die into physical expression, into acts. However,
there are places where the living spirit is instantly reborn,
where, in effect, the sacrifice kindles spirit.

Spirit *loves* to pour itself out,
to give itself as sacrifice in the physical.
When you know true gratitude you are acknowledging
     the sacrifice,
and recognizing the spirit.
Gratitude makes the earth fertile for spiritual sacrifice.
Gratitude calls to the spirit.
Gratitude is your slain/given spirit responding to the call
of the divine spirit from which it came forth.

~

A whole new dimension of communication
between the spiritual worlds
and your physical world is waiting to open up.
It *is* opening.
It *must* open.
The so-called dead are waiting,
as are the angels and the soldiers of light.
You have no idea how great their eagerness is,
how great their need and longing.
Your heart senses this,
open to it.
Turn to the spirit worlds,
so close and near,
open and ask.

~

All that I am is yours.

~

Be,
then you can *do.*